Kindheit – Bildung – Erziehung. Philosophische Perspektiven

Reihe herausgegeben von

Johannes Drerup, Institut für Allgemeine Erziehungswiss., Technische Universität Dortmund, Dortmund, Germany

Franziska Felder, Institut für Bildungswissenschaft, Universität Wien, Wien, Austria

Veronika Magyar-Haas, Departement Erziehungs- und Bildungswiss, Université Fribourg, Fribourg, Switzerland

Gottfried Schweiger, Ethik und Armutsforschung, Universität Salzburg, Salzburg, Austria

In der Reihe „Kindheit– Bildung – Erziehung: Philosophische Perspektiven" erscheinen Monographien und Sammelbände, die sich mit philosophischen Debatten über Fragen der Kindheit, der Bildung und der Erziehung beschäftigen. Thematisiert werden etwa Problematiken der theoretischen Konzeptualisierung, der Legitimation und Gewährleistung von Erziehung und Bildung in (post-) modernen Gesellschaften genauso wie aktuelle Kontroversen über normativ relevante Unterscheidungen zwischen Kindern und Erwachsenen, über spezifische Güter der Kindheit und über das Verhältnis von Eltern- und Kinderrechten in und außerhalb von liberalen Demokratien. Die Reihe richtet sich an Interessierte aus der Erziehungs- und Bildungsphilosophie, den Childhood Studies, der Philosophie der Kindheit und aus weiteren philosophischen Disziplinen (z.B. Politische Philosophie), die sich mit den genannten Themen- und Problemfeldern beschäftigen.

In the series "Childhood and Education. Philosophical Perspectives" monographs and edited volumes are published that deal with philosophical debates about childhood and education. Topics include philosophical questions and problems concerning the conceptualization, justification and the practice of education in (post-)modern societies, as well as controversies over normatively relevant distinctions between children and adults, the specific goods of childhood, and the relation between the rights of children and parents in and beyond liberal democracies. The series addresses scholars from the philosophy of education, childhood studies, philosophy of childhood as well as from other philosophical disciplines (e.g. political philosophy), who are interested in the aforementioned topics and issues.

More information about this series at https://link.springer.com/bookseries/16428

Graciela Tonon
Editor

Re-defining Children's Participation in the Countries of the South

1682
J.B. METZLER

Editor
Graciela Tonon
CICS-UP School of Social Sciences
University of Palermo
Buenos Aires, Argentina

ISSN 2662-5040 ISSN 2662-5059 (electronic)
Kindheit – Bildung – Erziehung. Philosophische Perspektiven
ISBN 978-3-662-64166-8 ISBN 978-3-662-64167-5 (eBook)
https://doi.org/10.1007/978-3-662-64167-5

Cover figure: © PeopleImages/Getty Images/iStock
Planning/Editing: Franziska Remeika
This J.B. Metzler imprint is published by the registered company Springer-Verlag GmbH, DE part of Springer Nature.
The registered company address is: Heidelberger Platz 3, 14197 Berlin, Germany

To my children Pedro and Erica and my husband Walter, for giving me their daily love and always supporting me.

Acknowledgments

To the authors who participated in this book

To the childrens who allow me to continue learning day after day.

To the Editors of the *Childhood and Education. Philosophical Perspectives Series*, Franziska Felder, Veronika Magyar-Haas, Johannes Drerup and Gottfried Schweiger, from Springer Nature—J. B. Metzler, who gives me the opportunity of editing this book.

To Elsa Zingman, Dean of the Faculty of Social Sciences of Universidad de Palermo, Argentina, who always encourages and supports my work.

Introduction

This book is the result of the work of authors who live/work in countries of the South, particularly in Latin America and Africa. Far from the idea that these two continents are separated by the immensity of the Atlantic Ocean, when considering the participation of boys and girls in each of them, we observe certain similarities and common concerns.

As early as 1993, Dogan and Pahré had pointed out that the first factor that separates research teams is ideology; making it clear that differences in methods or techniques, did not rank first. And in the case of the authors of this book, we are precisely united by our values and our ideas that consider children as true actors and protagonists of their life stories. We have discovered that beyond the diversity of our geographies, our histories and our cultures, the characteristics of the lives of our children and their real possibilities for participation, related us.

The book is composed by seven chapters dedicated to reflecting on the participation of boys and girls in the countries of the South.

The first chapter, by my own, begins by reviewing the concept of participation, its origins and development in Latin America, and particularly in South America. It then delves into the concept of participation on the basis of the Capability Approach. Next, it focuses on the specificities of the concept of children's participation, with a special emphasis on the situation of boys and girls in South America, including the results of a research in Argentina. For finally puts forth the capability approach as a theoretical proposal to study children's participation in South America.

The second chapter by Shazly Savahl and Sabirah Adams, from South Africa, considers the key elements of conducting participatory research with children, on children's subjective well-being in constrained social contexts. The authors deliberate on the methodological and ethical implications and put forward the Children's Delphi, an innovative participatory methodological framework, advancing children as the authentic knowers and experts on their lives. Children's Delphi provides a structured, ethics-focused approach to meaningful inclusion of children's views in research, practice and policy, being in this way important to consider the implications of conducting participatory policy research related to children.

The objective of chapter three, by Enrique Delamónica, Kenneth Ozoemenam & Annie Ekanem, analyses three instances of child participation in Nigeria that entail the practice of engaging with children and adolescents as part of the efforts by UNICEF to listen to their views about child poverty, understand adolescents' perspectives, and include their voices in UNICEF's work. It presents the results of a qualitative study carried out in all six geopolitical zones of Nigeria about what children think, feel, want, and expect about their situation, their role in the community, and their future to delves on efforts to institutionalize adolescents' voice and participation within UNICEF work and activities in Nigeria.

In chapter four, Damian Molgaray reflects on children's citizenship in the countries of South America, given that the literature that exists on this topic refers mainly to the situation of the countries of the North. The social and political phenomena that occurs in the southern countries show a particular reality that poses special meanings about citizenship: weak institutionalization processes and democratic transitions not yet consolidated, reveal provisional visions of children citizenship, visualizing experiences of agency operating in the margins.

Irma Eloff & Daniël Eloff in chapter five, present two cases in South Africa in which the basic rights of children were considered, but their participation was absent. The cases illustrate the possibilities of expanding the participation of children in legal proceedings within the scope of the national Constitution and reflect on the participation of children in education. It also considers how school closures and the national lockdown have amplified existing inequalities in the country. It highlights the importance of greater public awareness of quality education, the advancement of a collective responsibility for education, and a redefinition of the concept of school.

In chapter six Cornelia Walther points out that for participation to be meaningful to children, they must have an educational experience designed to systematically guide them to think critically and understand the impact their aspirations, emotions, thoughts, and feelings have on each other. She proposes Purpose for Power (P4P) a program to train teachers and caregivers that promotes a model that leads to genuine participation and hereby empowerment, from the inside out, considering that aspiration for meaning is the central driver of human decision making. It also presents the experience of education in Haiti in which P4P, a sustainable set of tools using local resources, and expertise to build lasting wellbeing, including mental and physical health, was used.

The final chapter of the book, by Claudia Mikkelsen, contributes to the debate of rurality expressed in the role of children as subjects with rights based on their opportunities of participation. It presents the results of a research with children living in rural areas in Argentina, focusing on the meaning and significance of inhabiting rural territories from their own voices.

I want to especially thank the authors who participated in this book based on their committed and innovative works, which make visible the need to advance in the path of promoting the participation of boys and girls on the planet but especially in the countries of the South.

July 2021.

Graciela H. Tonon

Contents

Editors and Contributors

About the Editor

Graciela Tonon, Director Research Centre in Social Sciences (CICS-UP) and Master Program in Social Sciences, School of Social Sciences, Universidad de Palermo, Argentina. Director UNICOM, School of Social Sciences, Universidad Nacional de Lomas de Zamora, Argentina.
gtonon1@palermo.edu

Contributors

Sabirah Adams, Language Development Group, Centre for Higher Education Development, University of Cape Town. South Africa.
sabirah.adams@uct.ac.za

Enrique Delamonica, Senior Adviser Statistics and Monitoring (Child Poverty and Gender Equality) Data & Analytics Section, Division of Data, Analytics, Planning & Monitoring, UNICEF.
edelamonica@unicef.org

Annie Maurice Ekanem Social Policy Officer, UNICEF, Nigeria.
aekanem@unicef.org

Daniël J. Eloff, Department of Law, Akademia, Pretoria, 0002, South Africa.
daniel@akademia.ac.za

Irma Eloff, Department of Educational Psychology, University of Pretoria, Pretoria, South Africa.
irma.eloff@up.ac.za

Claudia Andrea Mikkelsen, Member Research Project "Quality of life of 12 years old children in the Province of Buenos Aires", LOMASCYT, Universidad Nacional de Lomas de Zamora, Argentina. Researcher INHUS, CONICET, GESPYT, FHum, UNMdP-CIG, UNCPBA.
claudiamikkelsen@gmail.com

Damián Molgaray, Research Center in Social Sciences (CICS-UP) School of Social Sciences, Universidad de Palermo, Argentina.
damian.molgaray@gmail.com

Kenneth Ozoemenam, Social Policy Officer, UNICEF, Nigeria.
kozoemenam@gmail.com

Shazly Savahl, Centre for Interdisciplinary Studies of Children, Families and Society, University of the Western Cape. South Africa.
ssavahl@uwc.ac.za

Cornelia C. Walther, POZE Space; Deakin University, Australia; Muenster University, Germany.
8poze8@gmail.com, Web: www.poze.cc

Children's Participation in South America: A Proposal Based on the Capability Approach

1

Graciela Tonon

1.1 The Genealogy of the Concept of Participation in South America

The concept of participation features a prominent role in South America and in Latin America as well. It emerged in the 1970s within the context of new social and political practices, with the aim of paving the way for a social development process that might put an end to inequality and injustice in the region.

As a preliminary remark, it is worth noting that the concepts of South America and Latin America present their specificities. Gardino (2010, p. 12) argues that one of the most controversial issues is the difference between Latin America and South America as a geostrategic, social and cultural entity, with a shift to this latter position in the past few years. In this respect, academics and practitioners consider the concept of South America as able to forge political and economic projects as well as a common reinforced international projection. Gardini (2010, p. 26) expressed that, except for Europe, South America is "*the world's region where regionalism has a longer tradition and where it has achieved the most developed and sophisticated forms*". However, while in South America regionalism is an expression of unity and solidarity, under the alleged ideological affinity between administrations, South American regionalism is characterized by competing projects, whose rationalities and agendas are divergent (Gardini, 2010, p. 26). In addition, South America has a long tradition of participatory processes aimed at attaining social rights and overcoming situations of inequality and injustice. South America is a

G. Tonon (✉)
CICS-UP, School of Social Sciences, Universidad de Palermo, Buenos Aires, Argentina
e-mail: gtonon1@palermo.edu

G. Tonon (ed.), *Re-defining Children's Participation in the Countries of the South*, Kindheit – Bildung – Erziehung. Philosophische Perspektiven,
https://doi.org/10.1007/978-3-662-64167-5_1

particular region of our planet with a plurality of realities stemming from different dimensions, such as the political, social, psychological, cultural and economic ones (Tonon & Benatuil, 2019).

The concept of participation gained added impetus in the 1980s with the contributions of the ECLAC (Economic Commission for Latin America and the Caribbean). This included the work of Kadt (1982) who, in referring to community participation for health, distinguished between the so-called participation in the implementation of actions from the so-called participation in decision making. In 1985, ECLAC (pp. 4–5) prepared a document in which it summarized the essence of the concept of participation for Latin America. The document stated that participation was an act of individual will and that therefore it could not be imposed as an act of coercion, and further that a process could not be considered as participative if it did not allow individuals to decide not to participate.

However, in order for participation to be effective, it is necessary to go beyond the individual act and develop a collective and organized action taking the form of a collective decision. For this reason, citizen information and consultation concerning previously established programs cannot be considered as participation. The practice of participation entails a feeling of belonging and, at the same time, of taking action since, for the community to engage in authentic participation, it is essential to determine its degree of autonomy to intervene in the relevant process and introduce changes in the original design; in other words, the community must participate in equal conditions with those responsible for the project, whether they be agents of the central or the local government.

Subsequently, in the 1990s, Sirvent's work in Argentina made a significant contribution to the field. The author distinguished between real and symbolic participation. Participation is real when the members of an institution or group carry out actions that have an effective influence on all the processes of institutional life and on the nature of decisions, leading to changes in the existing power structures. Participation is symbolic when actions have little or no influence on institutional policies and management (2010, p. 64). According to Sirvent, symbolic participation creates in individuals and groups the illusion of exercising a non-existent power—it is the "as if" of participation (Sirvent, 1994).

It follows from the above that the different meanings ascribed to the notion of participation point to its significance as a human right and as an instrument that can enable the population to have an influence on the adoption and implementation of development decisions (ECLAC, 1985, p. 4).

1.2 Participation in the Late Twentieth Century and the Early Twenty-First Century

In order to define the concept of participation, Liebel and Saadi (2012) draw on Anderson's (1998, p. 574) statement that the term participation is a floating signifier. The authors add that this term takes a more specific meaning only when the objectives at stake are known, as well as the context and the conditions under which such objectives are established (Liebel & Saadi, 2012, p. 125).

In the last decade of the twentieth century and the first two decades of the twenty-first century, theoretical proposals about participation have been put forward in other locations that might prove useful when analyzing the South American context.

In her work on participation, White (1996–2004, pp. 145–148) ponders on two important dimensions: who participates and what is the level of participation. She distinguishes four types of participation: nominal, instrumental, representative and transformative. In the case of nominal participation, the interest of those who design and implement the programs is legitimation and the perspective of the participants is inclusion; in instrumental participation, the interest of those who design and implement the programs is efficiency and the perspective of the participants is cost; in representative participation, the interest of those who design and implement programs is sustainability and the perspective of the participants is leverage; and in transformative participation, the interest of those who design and implement development programs and the perspective of the participants is empowerment. Finally, White (2004, p. 154) suggests three steps in addressing the "non-politics" of participation: The recognition that participation is a political issue, the analysis of the interests represented in participation and the recognition that participation and non-participation, while they always reflect interests, do not do so in an open arena.

If we place the emphasis on the objectives of participation, and following Theis (2007), we can distinguish between an instrumental or utilitarian conception of participation, under which participation is regarded as a means, and a rights-based conception, which is transformative and emancipatory, and which perceives participation as an objective. Along these lines, Liebel and Saadi (2012, pp. 125–126) explain that the instrumental or utilitarian conception uses participation to make a measure more effective, involving those affected in the planning so that they can become more identified with it, or when the objective is to improve performance and thus it is turned into a personal matter. Conversely, rights-based participation is aimed at fostering emancipation and equal rights, thus contributing to the democratization of society and of social relations, with a transformative role toward achieving changes in the social and political structures. In this latter case, it is necessary to know what are the underlying interests and the specific conditions of execution in order to determine whether people can make use of their right to participation and whether participation makes sense for them.

Participation is the right to participate in political decisions that affect life, having to be a free, significant and complete right (Thede, 2009, p. 114). And this is so as "*regardless of how participation is understood, there is no doubt that it must be voluntary and based on mutual respect*" (Liebel & Saadi, 2012, p. 138).

1.3 Participation based on the Capability Approach

Amartya Sen's capability approach also explores the concept of participation, which is our focus of interest here. For Sen (2001, p. 19), "political and social participation has intrinsic value for human life and well-being. To be prevented from participation in the political life of the community is a major deprivation".

Sen (2000) advocates the capability approach as a theoretical proposal to assess life satisfaction, social situations and public policy design, with an impact on economic development, social policies and international development. According to Sen (2000), a person's capability refers to his/her actual ability to attain valuable life achievements, reflecting alternative combinations of functionings which that person can achieve. Functionings are defined as a representation of the things that a person values doing or being. This approach considers the relevance of the differences in people's satisfaction of their needs, focusing on the fact that people may need different resources for the development of the same freedoms. A significant aspect of freedom is that it makes us responsible for what we do, since a capability is the power to do something and the responsibility that this implies. The fundamental feature of capabilities, as active behaviors, is that they are valuable actions, structured not only on the basis of needs or rights but also on the basis of values (Hoevel, 2011). From this perspective, people's lives are viewed in an inclusive way (Sen, 2009).

Sen (1999) argues that individual freedom can be considered a central value in social appraisal and an integral product of social arrangements, with far-reaching implications on the assessment of social institutions and political decisions. From Sen's (2000, p. 35) perspective, individuals are conceived as active agents of change, rather than as mere recipients of benefits. Sen advocates using the term "agent" in its older sense, according to which an individual acts and brings about changes, and whose achievements can be judged in terms of his/her own values and objectives, regardless of any assessment in terms of external criteria (Sen, 2000, p. 34). Under this approach, individuals are no longer passive recipients of actions produced by governmental bodies and professional teams, but instead actors and protagonists of processes in development. People are thus seen as agents with capabilities focused on the substantive freedom to lead a life they have reason to value and expand the real options from which they can choose (Sen, 2000, p. 350). A person's capabilities also depend on the nature of social arrangements, which can be crucial for individual freedoms. In this sense, the state and society cannot evade their responsibility (Sen, 2000, p. 345).

Building on Sen's approach, Crocker (2014, pp. 100–102), in making reference to participation for local development, distinguishes different modes of group decision making, identifying seven types of participation, namely nominal participation, where a person is a member of a group but does not attend decision-making meetings; passive participation, where group members attend decision-making meetings, but listen passively to reports about the decisions made by others; consultative participation, where members provide information and give their opinion, but it is the leaders the ones who decide; petitionary participation, where members petition authorities to make certain decisions and do certain things, usually to remedy injustices; participatory implementation, where the leaders make the decisions and the members only implement those decisions; bargaining, where all parties involved seek to strike a final deal; and deliberative participation, where both members and leaders deliberate together and examine proposals and reasons in order to reach agreements that at least a majority can accept. Crocker concludes that the further one goes down this list, the deeper is the participatory mode in the sense of an individual or collective agency (Crocker, 2014, p. 102).

However, as noted by Liebel and Saadi (2012, p. 132): "*Participation is not transformative* per se, *as it can be used for integrative purposes or to maintain power*". Along these lines, Drydyk (2005) also warns that while it is usually understood that participation takes place in a democratic setting, there are certain situations in which participation is not democratic. The author argues that participatory schemes sometimes reproduce social inequalities within communities. Thus, some actors have less voice than others as they are inevitably dominated by socially and economically more powerful groups, who finally are the ones that obtain more benefits.

As to the modes in which decision-making participation is combined with weak forms of participation, Drydyk (2005, pp. 259–260) identified seven proposals: passive participation, which takes place when a person is told what is happening; participation in information giving; participation by consultation, when someone is consulted and others listen to his/her opinions; participation for material incentives, such as providing labor for food or cash; functional participation, to meet certain objectives after decisions have been made; interactive participation, which leads to action plans and the formation of new local institutions or the strengthening of existing ones; and self-mobilization, when people spontaneously take initiatives independent of institutions in order to change the system.

In line with the above, and as stated by Sen (1999, p. 76) "the most important social obligation must include the fundamental participation rights that enable citizens to describe and decide their values and priorities".

From our point of view, the essence of participation lies in joint decision making, which implies a distribution of power rather than merely acting together (Tonon, 2020).

1.4 Children's Participation

Before turning to the study of children's participation, it is necessary to acknowledge that childhood is a social construction that varies over time and space.

In his work on childhood, Sanchez (2004, p. 19) points out that the study of childhood requires two levels of analysis, as each childhood model must be understood and explained by reference to the model of society that has produced it, along with the events, actions and relationships that produce it, and also by reference to how children as subjects of relationships operate, influence and interpret those actions and relationships. It is thus necessary to conceive this stage of life as a present state, in which multiple factors converge from which a particular form of child being emerges, with its own problematics and expectations derived from the social, cultural and economic context in which children construct their biographies (Mieles Barrera & Tonon, 2015, p. 30).

Closely interlinked with the above, it is worth discussing two concepts developed by Freire (1970–2005, p. 125) in connection with time and space. Freire defines the concept of "epochal unit" as the complex of ideas, concepts, values, hopes, doubts and challenges in dialectical interaction with their opposites and argues that then the "thematic universe" is the complex of interacting themes of an epoch. In this respect, Freire (1970–2005, p. 128) points out that any given society, within its epochal unit, contains its own particular themes, in addition to any existing universal themes. And in the case of children's participation, such participation relates to the discovery and knowledge of the place that each society gives to children and adults, as in some cultures children are seen as a separate group, while in others they are considered, rather than in terms of their age, in terms of the real possibilities they have of taking part in community life (Liebel & Saadi, 2012, p. 128).

In addition, participation is always intertwined with relationships and interrelationships; therefore, children must be understood and respected not only as executive actors, but also as subjects capable of thinking and acting, with rights of their own (Liebel & Saadi, 2012, p. 138).

In this connection, Malone and Hartug (2010, p. 26) warn that "*children's participation is often defined in terms of the roles that adults ascribe to children, as though children cannot participate in decision making or contribute to society unless they are formally engaged through adult-initiated projects.*"

If we chart the history of the concept of children's participation, we can find the work by Hart (1992), who adapted Arnstein's "Ladder of Participation" to children's participation, defining participation as the process of sharing decisions which affect children's life and the life of the community in which they live. It is worth noting that Arnstein constructed the ladder of participation in 1969 and it still retains considerable contemporary relevance. At the top of the ladder is citizen control, and at the bottom is the category of "non-participation" characterized by manipulation. "Arnstein's point of departure is the citizen on the receiving end of projects; she draws a distinction between 'citizen power', which includes citizen control, delegated power and partnership, and 'tokenism', in which she includes consultation, informing and placation" (Cornwall, 2008, p. 270).

A decade later, Moses (2008, p. 328) addressed the concept of children's participation and raised four questions: participation by whom? In what? For what purpose? Under what conditions? The author argues that children's participation takes place in two dimensions: the private or personal dimension, focused on the household and family; and the public dimension, which comprises the community, school and government. While Moses recognizes that the study of these dimensions is usually undertaken separately, she states that they should in fact be approached in an integrated manner. According to the author (2008, p. 339), the role played by the environments (family, local, national and global) is crucial in the study of children's participatory processes, as the interactions between the interventions and the environments are key to understanding the barriers to participation. No participatory process can be analyzed in isolation of the societal forces operating within it.

Linares Pontón and Velez (2007, p. 224) state that the promotion of children's participation through concrete actions that improve their lives and those of the members of their communities is a strategy aimed at the transformation of the democratic culture of both children and their community, and where children are conceived as social subjects capable of contributing to the transformation of their environment. It is thus necessary to promote children's involvement in decision-making processes, foster the participation of the community in issues worrying children and create learning spaces in which children and adults can acquire abilities for responsible participation (Linares Pontón & Velez 2007, p. 230).

Participation occurs in informal as well as formal settings, and adults who seek to facilitate children's participation need to begin by understanding where it already occurs (Chawla, 2001, p. 3). Chawla proposes seven different forms of participation: prescribed participation, assigned participation, invited participation, negotiated participation, self-initiated negotiated participation, graduated participation and collaborative participation. In prescribed participation, the child feels a moral and cultural obligation to participate and considers the opportunity to do so as a privilege. In assigned participation, it is the adults who provide opportunities for participation to the child; however, the child experiences this situation as meaningful. Invited participation is initiated and controlled by an adult, but the child has the right to withdraw without feeling disadvantaged. In negotiated participation, the child is assigned a participatory role, but has opportunities to negotiate how to carry it out. In self-initiated negotiated participation, the child initiates and controls his/her participation by negotiating its level, type and duration. Graduated participation occurs as the child increases his/her competence, has the opportunity to practice new types of participation, assume new levels of responsibility and find new opportunities for meaningful participation in the community. Finally, collaborative participation is initiated and supported by a group, which collectively negotiates the level and form of participation (Chawla, 2001, p. 3).

Chawla (2001, p. 5) summarized the conclusions of the members of a symposium that took place in Oslo on "Children's Participation in Community Settings" stating that there is no "one size fits all" model for children's participation that can be applied across all community settings, social groups and cultural contexts; participation needs to be fostered across a broad range of formal and informal settings; the qualities that characterize participatory processes that respect children's dignity and competence can be specified and documented; and that creating processes of this kind benefits not only children, but also their communities and societies.

> Participation is a process in which children and youth engage with other people around issues that concern their individual and collective life conditions. Participants interact in

> ways that respect each other's dignity, with the intention of achieving a shared goal. In the process, the child experiences itself as playing a useful role in the community. Formal processes of participation deliberately create structures for children's engagement in constructing meaning and sharing decision making. (Chawla, 2001, p. 1)

However, in order to design child participation strategies, account must also be taken of children's social position and of how the general economic patterns condition or determine that position. This does not merely entail modernizing traditional societies but rather analyzing how to define social equality and justice and how to put them in practice in different societies (Liebel & Saadi, 2012, pp. 137).

All of the above requires changes in the societal structures in order to strengthen children's position and enhance their participation.

> It is insufficient to simply provide opportunities for children to have their say or participate in adult structures and processes. They should be provided with an opportunity to challenge and change these structures and processes by negotiating their own forms of participation. We argue that authentic participation involves inclusion – wherein the system changes to accommodate the participation and values of children. (Percy-Smith & Malone, 2001, p. 42)

Child participation can take various forms of involvement, engagement and commitment, and not all child participation is active, social, purposeful, meaningful or constructive. Authentic child participation starts with children themselves, on their own terms, within their own realities and in pursuit of their own visions, dreams, hopes and concerns. Children need information, support and favorable conditions in order to participate appropriately and in a way that enhances their dignity and self-esteem (UNICEF, 2003, p. 5).

Liebel and Saadi (2012, p. 127) propose understanding participation as both a mode of individualization—greater freedom—and of socialization—a greater belonging—and placing particular emphasis on the relationship between both perspectives. This is closely connected with the fact that participation preserves children's dignity (Melton, 1999).

1.5 The Study of Children's Participation in South America Based on the Capability Approach

Melton (1999) noted that, in the history of children's rights, the tradition of child protection has been stronger than the tradition that emphasizes children's agency and rights to self-determination and personal expression.

The main aim of this chapter is to gain further insights into children's participation in South America on the basis of the capability approach. For such purpose, a bibliographic search was carried out to identify publications applying the capability approach to children's participation in countries in the region. The search included a review of the *Journal of Human Development and Capabilities*, the official journal of the *Human Development and Capability Association* and the list of bibliography compiled by the *Human Development and Capability Association* per year, which gathers publications from its members. The search did not return any results on publications applying the capability approach to children's participation in South American countries.

In order to explore children's participation in South America on the basis of the capability approach, it is worth recalling that Sen stated that (1999, p. 4) "...capabilities that adults enjoy are deeply conditional on their experience as children". For Sen (2009, p. 17), the capability approach proposes a change from concentrating on the *means* of living to the *actual opportunities* of living in itself. The path of capabilities development followed by an individual combines elements of freedom with unfreedoms, due to path dependencies. A new horizon for the capability approach is therefore established when the focus of analysis is placed on children's capabilities (Comim et al., 2011).

In line with this notion, Biggeri et al. (2006) recognize that children have capabilities that are specific to the phases of their life. The relevance of these capabilities can vary according to age and even to gender. Childhood is complex and constituted by different sensitive periods and some capabilities can be more "relevant" as age increases (Biggeri et al., 2006, p. 66).

Biggeri (2004, pp. 6–9) devised an open-ended list of children's capabilities—following Robeyns' (2003) proposal—in which he included the capability of participation. The others are: physical health, love and care, mental well-being, bodily integrity and safety, social relations, education, freedom from economic and non-economic exploitation, shelter and environment, leisure activities, respect, religion and identity, time-autonomy and mobility.

During 2017–2018, I directed a research project in different towns of the Province of Buenos Aires, Argentina, focused on children's well-being. It was a quantitative research study,[1] using the ISCWeB, a questionnaire created by *Children's Worlds*, an international research network that studies children's well-being all over the world (Tonon, 2018). The sample was composed by 680 children, 46% boys and 54% girls, aged 12–13 years old. The instrument included some questions, phrases and scales in reference to children's participation about: their rights, their opinions listened to and taken into account by adults, their participation in decision making together with adults and their freedom.

When we asked children if they knew **what rights they had**, 70.3% answered in the affirmative, while 3.6% reported not knowing their rights and 25.8% reported not being sure whether they knew their rights. When asked if they knew the Convention on the Rights of the Child, 31.2% answered in the affirmative, while 20.8% reported not knowing the Convention and 47.8% said they were not sure whether they knew it.

As to the children's responses in connection with **having their opinions listened to and taken into account by adults,** the results show that:

[1] Research Project "Quality of Life of 12 years old Children in Buenos Aires Province" (2017/18). LomasCyT Program, Universidad Nacional de Lomas de Zamora, Argentina.

- With respect to parents, 48% of the children stated that they are always listened to, 28.5% reported that they are almost always listened to, 11.9% stated that they are sometimes listened to, 7.7% said they are only occasionally listened to, and 3.9% stated that they are not listened to.
- With respect to teachers, 22.9% said that they are always listened to, 30.4% stated that they are almost always listened to, 3.7% reported that they are sometimes listened to, 14.4% stated that they are only occasionally listened to, and 8,6% said that they are not listened to.
- With respect to the children's level of satisfaction with being listened to by adults, the median was 7.94 (on a 0–10 scale).

With respect to the children's **participation in decision making together with adults,** the following results were obtained:

- As to participation in their families, 40.9% of the children reported always participating; 24.1%, almost always; 18.1%, sometimes; 7.5%, only occasionally; and 9.4% responded that they do not participate.
- As to participation at school: 31.6% of the children reported always participating; 30.9%, almost always; 18.8%, sometimes; 10.3%, only occasionally; and 8.3% stated that they do not participate.
- As to participation in the neighborhood: 16.4% of the children reported always participating; 14.3%, almost always; 15.9%, sometimes; 13.4%, only occasionally; and 40% stated that they do not participate.
- As to participation in the country: 12.1% of the children reported always participating; 19.5%, almost always; 26.9%, sometimes; 24.8%, only occasionally; and 16.7% stated that they do not participate.

With respect to the children's level of **satisfaction with the freedom** they enjoy, the median was 8.12 (on a 0–10 scale).

A brief analysis of the above results reveals that:

- There is a noticeable difference between the percentage of children that report knowing their rights and those that report knowing the Convention on the Rights of the Child.
- Parents listen to and take into account children's opinions in a higher percentage than teachers.
- In addition, it is worth noting that, when it comes to children's possibilities to make decisions together with adults and participate in those processes, the percentage decreases considerably as one moves from the family to the school, the community and the country, in other words, from the micro- to the macro-level.

In referring to social participation, Comim et al. (2011, p. 12) note that it is a term that implies something more than mere action: It implies that action is public, visible in the whole society or community, as well as in particular interactive situations. In other words, social means visible for everybody. The authors point out that the participation of children in the different social contexts implies the consideration of: children's competencies, resources and capabilities, which are linked to the possibility of being acted out, understood and recognized as significant; the environmental conditions that allow their expression and need to be valued so that they are reproduced over time and the different cultures in which capabilities are built, which can only be considered if they are made visible together with the practices and orientations that inspire them (Comim et al. 2011, p. 12)

> Children's social participation needs to be visible in public contexts in order to clearly manifest their citizenship and their inclusion in a society that incorporates the full range of rights and opportunities found in the self-determination human rights approach. (Freeman 1998, quoted in Biggeri & Santi, 2012, p. 389)

Thus, the possibility of children's real participation in their households and community settings may lead to what Hodgett (2008, p. 174) calls the expansion of capabilities and the widening of the capability set.

Chawla (2001, p. 4) proposes the concept of meaningful participation, which entails a developmental perspective that will change depending upon children's interests, goals and sense of their own capabilities, as well as their societies' expectations regarding appropriate tasks and accomplishments.

1.6 Conclusions

Children's participation must be analyzed taking into consideration the time and space in which it is developed, as each society constructs its notion of childhood in social and historical terms.

We agree with Liebel and Saadi (2012, p. 138) when they state that children's participation not only implies being heard and being able to give opinions, but it also entails an active and daily participation in vital economic and social processes, which can shape new horizons for children's position in society. Along the same lines, children's participation must diversify and become an element of social vindication, as children are subjects that have been historically excluded (Save the Children, Redlamyc and IIN 2013, p. 12).

In focusing our analysis on South America, as it mentioned before, this region has a long tradition of participatory processes aimed at attaining social rights and overcoming situations of inequality and injustice.

In the case that we analyze from Argentina, it can be seen that regarding the possibilities that children have to make joint decisions with adults and to participate in these processes, the percentage decreases considerably, in a way that goes from the family, to the school, to the community and to the country, that is, from the micro- to the macro-level.

Child participation must be authentic and meaningful. Most of all, authentic and meaningful child participation requires a radical shift in adult thinking and behavior—from an exclusionary to an inclusionary approach to children and their capabilities (UNICEF, 2003, p. 4).

From our point of view, the essence of participation lies in joint decision making, which implies a distribution of power rather than merely acting together. In this connection, applying the capability approach to the analysis of the reality of children's participation in our region is particularly important, as children's participation, along with that of adults, can influence the design of more inclusive and co-responsible public policies.

Thus, further research and work needs to be undertaken to enable children to participate in their own affairs and to generate knowledge that allows understanding their situation and society's more global issues, considered from their own realities and perceptions (Mieles Barrera & Tonon, 2015, p. 29).

And this is precisely so because, as argued by Sen (2000), participation in political and social decisions cannot be seen as means to human development, but must be understood as constitutive parts of the ends of human development in themselves.

References

Anderson, G. (1998). Toward authentic participation: Deconstructing the discourses of participatory reforms in education. *American Educational Research Journal, 35*(4), 571–603.

Arnstein, S. (1969). A ladder of citizen participation. *JAIP, 35*(4), 216–224.

Biggeri, M. (2004). 'Capability approach and child well-being', invited paper at the International Conference Promoting Human Rights and Social Policies for Children Conceptualizing their Capabilities and Women: Monitoring and Achieving the Millennium Development Goals, UNICEF The New School University, New York, 28–30 April.

Biggeri, M., Libanora, R., Mariani, S., & Menchini, L. (2006). Children conceptualizing their capabilities: Results of a survey conducted during the first children's world congress on child labour. *Journal of Human Development, 7*(1), 59–83. https://doi.org/10.1080/14649880500501179

Biggeri, M., & Santi, M. (2012). The missing dimensions of children's well-being and well-becoming. *Journal of Human Development and Capabilities, 13*(3), 373–395.

Chawla, L. (2001). Evaluating children's participation: Seeking areas of consensus. *PLA Notes, 42*(October), 9–13.

Comim, F., Ballet, J., Mario Biggeri, M., & Iervese, V. (2011). Introduction – Theoretical foundations and the book's roadmap. In M. Biggeri, J. Ballet, & F. Comim, (Eds.), *Children and the capability approach* (pp. 3–21). Palgrave Macmillan.

Cornwall, A. (2008). Unpacking 'Participation': models, meanings and practices. & Oxford University Press and Community Development Journal. https://doi.org/10.1093/cdj/bsn010. Advance Access Publication 5 June 2008.

Crocker, D. (2014). Participación deliberativa en el desarrollo local. In M. Nebel, P. Flores-Crespo, & M. T. Herrera (Ed.), *Desarrollo como libertad en América Latina. Fundamentos y aplicaciones* (pp. 97–125). Universidad Iberoamericana.

de Kadt, E. (1982). Participación de la comunidad para la salud. *Boletín de Planificación N° 14*. Santiago de Chile, Instituto latinoamericano de planificación económica y social- ILPES, pp. 53–70.

Drydyk, J. (2005). When is development more democratic? *Journal of Human Development, 6*(2), 247–267. https://doi.org/10.1080/14649880500120566

ECLAC (Comisión Económica para América Latina y el Caribe). (1985). Participación comunitaria, Estado y desarrollo hacia la incorporación de la dimensión participativa en la formulación y ejecucion de programas de desarrollo. https://repositorio.cepal.org/bitstream/handle/11362/35677/S8500484_es.pdf?sequence=1&isAllowed=y.
Freire, P. (1970–2005). *Pedagogía del oprimido*. Siglo XXI Editores.
Gardini, G. L. (2010). Proyectos de integración regional sudamericana: hacia una teoría de convergencia regional. Relaciones Internacionales, núm. 15, octubre de 2010 GERI – UAM, pp. 11–31. https://repositorio.uam.es/bitstream/handle/10486/678124/RI_15_2.pdf?sequence=1.
Hart, R. (1992). *Children's participation: From tokenism to citizenship*. UNICEF.
Hodgett, S. (2008). Sen, culture and expanding participatory capabilities in Northern Ireland. *Journal of Human Development and Capabilities, 9*(2), 165–183.
Hoevel, C. (2011). La teoría de la justicia de Amartya Sen y los orígenes del concepto católico de justicia social en Antonio Rosmini. *Revista Cultura Económica Año XXIX, Nº 81/82*: 38–53. https://repositorio.uca.edu.ar/bitstream/123456789/2068/1/teoria-justicia-amartya-sen.pdf.
Liebel, M., & Saadi, I. (2012). La participación infantil ante el desafío de la diversidad cultural. *Desacatos, 39, mayo-agosto* 2012, 123–140.
Linares Ponton, M. E., & Velez, H. (2007). Las niñas y los niños como agentes de cambio social. In Y. Corona Caraveo & M. E. Linares Pontón (Eds.), *Participación infantil y juvenil en América Latina*. Universidad Autónoma Metropolitana.
Malone, K., & Hartug, C. (Eds.) (2010). Challenges of participatory practice with children. In B. Percy-Smith & N. Thomas (Ed.), *A Handbook of Children and Young People's Participation. Perspectives from Theory and Practice* (pp. 24–38). Taylor and Francis Group.
Melton, G. B. (1999). Parents and children: Legal reform to facilitate children's participation. *American Psychologist, 54*(11), 935–944. https://doi.org/10.1037/h0088201
Mieles Barrera, M. D., & Tonon, G. (2015). *Calidad de vida y niñez, perspectivas desde la investigación cualitativa*. Universidad del Magdalena.
Moses, S. (2008). Children and participation in South Africa: An overview. *International Journal of Children's Rights, 16*, 327–342.
Percy-Smith, B., & Malone, K. (2001). Making children's participation in neighborhood settings relevant to the everyday lives of young people. *PLA Notes, 2001*(42), 18–22.
Robeyns, I. (2003). *The capability approach: An interdisciplinary introduction*. Curso previo a la Tercera Conferencia del Capability Approach, Pavia, Italia, 6 de Septiembre, pp. 1–57.
Sanchez, J. (2004). *Orfandades infantiles y adolescentes. Introducción a una sociología de la infancia*. Universidad Politécnica Salesiana, Save the Children (Suecia) Ediciones ABY-YALA.
Save the Children, Redlamyc e IIN. (2013). *La participación de niños, niñas y adolescentes en espacios de incidencia regional*. Documento de trabajo. Junio. Reflexiones y aprendizajes sobre la participación de niños, niñas y adolescentes en espacios de incidencia regional. Proyecto Regional protagonistas. Participación de niños, niñas y adolescentes en la construcción de sociedades inclusivas y democráticas, Montevideo. http://educacion.redlamyc.org/wp-content/uploads/2019/02/participacion_nnya.pdf.
Sen, A. (2001). La democracia como valor universal. *ISTOR Año, 1*(4), 10–28.
Sen, A. (1999). *La libertad individual como compromiso social*. Ediciones Abya-Ayala.
Sen, A. (2000). *Desarrollo y libertad*. Bogotá. Editorial Planeta.
Sen, A. (2009). *The idea of justice*. The Belknap Press of Harvard University Press.
Sirvent, M. T. (1994). *Educación de adultos: Investigación y Participación. Desafíos y Contradicciones*. Coquena.
Sirvent, M. T. (2010). La investigación acción participativa y la animación socio-cultural. Su papel en la participación ciudadana. *ATPS, 2010* (1), 61–74.
Thede, N. (2009). Decentralization, democracy and human rights: A human rights-based analysis of the impact of local democratic reforms on development. *Journal of Human Development and Capabilities, 10*(1), 103–123. https://doi.org/10.1080/14649880802675317
Theis, J. (2007). Performance, responsibility and political decision-making: Child and youth participation in Southeast Asia, East Asia and the Pacific. *Children, Youth and Environments Vol. 17, No. 1, Pushing the Boundaries: Critical International Perspectives on Child and Youth*

Participation – Focus on Southeast Asia, East Asia, the Pacific, South and Central Asia, and Japan pp. 1–13. University of Cincinnati. https://www.jstor.org/stable/, https://doi.org/10.7721/chilyoutenvi.17.1.0001.
Tonon, G. (2018). Directora de proyecto. *Calidad de vida de niños y niñas de 12 años en la Provincia de Buenos Aires*. Programa LomasCyT- Universidad Nacional de Lomas de Zamora, Argentina (2017–2018).
Tonon, G. (2020). *PENSAR A PARTICIPAÇÃO NA AMÉRICA LATINA A PARTIR DA PROPOSTA TEÓRICA DE AMARTYA SEN*. REVISTA REFLEXÕES, FORTALEZA-CE–Ano 9, Nº 17, Julho a Dezembro de 2020, pp. 140–149.
UNICEF. (2003). *The state of the world's children 2003*. UNICEF. https://www.unicef.org/sowc03/contents/pdf/SOWC03-eng.pdf.
White, S. (2004). Depoliticizing development: The uses and abuses of participation. In D. Eade (Ed.), *Development, NGOs, and civil society*. First published by Oxfam GB.

2 Conducting Participatory Research on Children's Subjective Well-Being: At the Interface of Ethics and Methods

Shazly Savahl and Sabirah Adams

2.1 Introduction

The concept of subjective well-being (SWB) has its genesis in the Greek philosophical concept of 'hedonia'. Hedonic well-being focuses on life satisfaction, happiness and SWB; it is often denoted as 'feeling well', representing the good life, and concretized as experiencing happiness (Adler & Seligman, 2016; Huta & Ryan, 2010). The hedonic constructs of happiness and SWB present with substantial conceptual overlap and are frequently used interchangeably in the literature (Camfield & Skevington, 2008; Medvedev & Landhuis, 2018).

SWB is a multifaceted expansive concept, which consists of the cognitive and affective perceptions, experiences, reflections, and appraisals that people ascribe toward their lives (Diener, 1984). The cognitive component refers to global and domain-based life satisfaction, while the affective component refers to positive affect (PA) and negative affect (NA) (Diener et al., 1999). These components are conceptualized on a 'tripartite' hierarchical structure that are conceptually aligned and moderately correlated (Diener, 2009). While the tripartite structure is the most widely used conceptualization of SWB, Busseri and Sadava (2011) have identified five structural conceptualizations of SWB commonly used in empirical studies. While the early history of social indicators of well-being has focused on adult populations, the last two decades have seen increased attention afforded to children's

S. Savahl (✉)
Centre for Interdisciplinary Studies of Children, Families and Society, University of the Western Cape, Cape Town, South Africa
e-mail: ssavahl@uwc.ac.za

S. Adams
Centre for Higher Education Development, University of Cape Town, Cape Town, South Africa
e-mail: sabirah.adams@uct.ac.za

G. Tonon (ed.), *Re-defining Children's Participation in the Countries of the South*, Kindheit – Bildung – Erziehung. Philosophische Perspektiven,
https://doi.org/10.1007/978-3-662-64167-5_2

well-being. Considering the structure of children's SWB, Savahl et al. (2021) proffer a quadripartite conceptualization, consisting of global and domain-based cognitive life satisfaction, and PA and NA. Alternative conceptualizations of children's SWB that offer a less structural approach and more aligned to the discursive tradition or post-structural turn (Fattore 2020) in the social sciences is also evident in the literature. Savahl et al. (2015b) advance the idea that SWB should be understood in relation to the dominant discourse of childhood in society. They perceive childhood as an ideologically configured construction—subsequently, how children assign meaning to their position in society, how they make sense of their role as a child and their social identity implicates how they perceive, experience and evaluate their lives in general and various aspects of their lives. From this perspective, children's SWB is by no means fixed or static but open and constantly shifting—there is a constant shaping, reshaping, contesting and negotiating of the meanings assigned to childhood, with SWB conceived of as an intersubjectively negotiated construct. A more detailed and well-considered narrative of the discursive position is provided by Fattore (2020) in his delineation of the praxeological shift in well-being research with children. He argues that well-being is less about 'a state that is achieved, but emotional experiences that are expressions of social practices, through which a subject position associated with a sense of well-being emerges' (Fattore 2020, p. 152; see also Fegter, 2014).

Taking the above into consideration, we can work toward a definition of children's SWB as a multidimensional construct consisting of the cognitive and affective perceptions and evaluations that children make about their lives in general and specific aspects of their lives (Savahl et al., 2019). When we ask children about their SWB, we are essentially asking them to appraise the extent to which they are satisfied with their lives in general, with certain aspects of their lives, and how they 'feel' about their lives, both in terms of positive and negative emotions.

Over the past decade, there have been substantial methodological advances in the measurement of children's SWB. Researchers have proceeded in two directions. The first and most dominant is the development of standardized scales and measures, often adapted from adult versions. Many of these instruments have demonstrated appropriate psychometric properties for use with specific populations, and some showing evidence of cross-cultural comparison (Casas & Rees, 2015; see also Proctor et al., 2009, for a review of life satisfaction measures developed for use with children and youth).

A considerable body of evidence exists in the international literature emphasizing that high levels of well-being are associated with a range of positive psycho-social outcomes in children (Holte et al., 2014; Moore et al., 2004; September & Savahl, 2009). Similarly, programs to increase children's level of well-being have shown to have a significant positive influence on their development trajectories and ultimately have a direct impact on the socio-economic success of nations. This rapidly developing area of empirical, theoretical, and social policy research, along with a committed and sustained advocacy agenda, has become known as the Child Indicator Movement (Ben-Arieh, 2008). The Movement has its genesis in the progression of children's rights legislation (most notably the United

Nations Convention on the Rights of the Child [UNCRC]), and the epistemological shift encapsulated in innovative epistemological and theoretical advancements in studies of children and childhood initially proposed by James and Prout (1990). It is through this epistemological shift that childhood is regarded as a valid structural feature of society and children's perspectives acknowledged as valid, their experiences as real, with the capacity to meaningfully reflect on their lives. The methodological upshot is that children transitioned from being absent in social research, to being objects of research, to being subjects of research. The focus on understanding these subjective positions ignited the interest in researching children's (subjective) well-being. Ultimately, this provided the momentum for the advancement of child-centered research, which gave rise to participatory methodologies. It is now widely accepted that children's participation should be foregrounded within the research process.

In this chapter, we consider the key elements of conducting participatory research with children on children's SWB in constrained social contexts. We highlight the importance of grounding participatory research in a child rights framework. We further deliberate on the methodological and ethical implications and put forward the Children's Delphi, an innovative participatory methodological framework, advancing children as the authentic knowers and authoritative experts on their lives. We contend that the Children's Delphi provides a structured and ethically focused approach for the meaningful inclusion of children's views in research, practice and policy. Finally, we consider the implications of conducting participatory research on social policies relating to children.

2.2 Considering Children's Participation

Child participation provides a critical framework for the inclusion of children in research, challenging previous models of children's research controlled by privileged and powerful adults (Fattore et al., 2012; 2017). It places the child centrally in the research process, with the aim of gaining a detailed understanding of their subjective experiences and meaning-making processes, while considering their social, cultural, and historical contexts (Fattore et al., 2007). The researcher's role in child participation shifts from the adult-centric perspective, working instead as a collaborator in ways that enhance the power children have over their own lives (Langhout & Thomas, 2010). Grounded in the theoretical and methodological assertions of the 'new sociology of childhood', child participation research has its genesis in international legislation on children's rights, most notably the UNCRC.

With early impetus in the Geneva Declaration on the Rights of the Child, which was drafted in 1924 and adopted by the League of Nations in 1934, children's rights legislation has advanced through a number of versions culminating in the United Nations Declaration of the Rights of the Child in 1959; and eventually in the UNCRC in 1989. The UNCRC consists of 54 articles guaranteeing children socio-economic and participation rights that confirm their position as rights' holders and valid members of society. The ratification of the treaty places an obligation on States parties to ensure its enactment. Governments are thus bound in international law to put children first and develop legislation and policies to ensure that the rights enshrined in the Convention are actioned. The UNCRC has four overarching guiding principles, which have implications for conducting research with children, namely:

- Non-discrimination
- Best interests of the child
- Survival and development
- The right to participation

The fourth guiding principle, the right to participation, is the most relevant in the context of the current chapter. It is most explicitly embedded in Article 12 of the UNCRC, which states that children have the right to freely express their opinion, to be heard, and have their opinions taken seriously on all matters that affect them (United Nations General Assembly, 1989). Article 13 further supports child participation in the form of freedom of expression—this includes the right to seek, receive, or impart information and ideas through the child's preferred form of communication. Through the collaborative methodologies of child participation research, children have contributed valuable knowledge around issues relating to their lives, including children's experiences of the natural environment, self-concept, labor, schooling, play, gender, sexuality and spirituality, and developing indicators of children's well-being (Adams & Savahl, 2017a, b; Adams et al., 2017; Benninger & Savahl 2017a, b; Mason & Watson, 2014; September & Savahl, 2009).

As Cuevas-Parra et al. (2016) note, the wealth of literature on child participation literature affords a number of models of child participation. Among these are Hart's Ladder of Participation, Treseder's Degrees of Participation, Shier's Pathways to Participation, Lansdown's Model of Participation, and Lundy's Model of Participation. More recently, McKendrick (2014) put forward a model, *Factors contributing to child well-being: A conceptual framework to situate place in context.* This model is 'context-focused' and provides a conceptual framework to understand the influence of children's neighborhood on their well-being. He developed a tool to expound the influence of place on children's overall well-being, in addition to his conceptual framework of place well-being. His tool, 'The impact of places on the well-being of children' is analogous to Hart's (1997) ladder of children's participation. It comprises a continuum ranging from the lowest rung, referred to as *damaging*, to the highest rung, transforming. Further, relevant to low- and middle-income contexts, Häkli and Kallio (2018) argue for the focus on children's 'political agency' by focusing on the 'phenomenology of political action' rather than more complex ontologies of the political.

Participation is considered necessary for citizenship, and alternatively is employed as a method to attain 'full citizenship' (Hultgren & Johannson, 2018).

Lundy (2007) critically avers that acknowledging and venerating children's views is not only a legally binding requirement (for States parties that have ratified the UNCRC), but also good pedagogical practice. In recent years, the operationalization of child participation has been debated in varying cross-cultural contexts that have adopted the UNCRC (Ansell, 2016; Lundy, 2007; Rye & Vold, 2018; Skelton, 2010). The key premise of these debates is the delineation of 'authentic participation' across different spheres that affect children's lives. The specific wording of Article 12 of the UNCRC has been a point of concern given that the emphasis on children's participation is associated with their age, 'Parties shall assure to the child who is capable of forming his or her own views the right to express those views freely in all matters affecting the child...' (United Nations General Assembly, 1989). Clark and Richards (2017) thus note that participation is oft considered to be enacted by individuals that are competent, responsible, and reflexive; essentially well-becoming (Ben-Arieh, 2008).

Fattore et al. (2018) point to the dearth of empirical endeavors exploring the challenges in incorporating children's participation within the research process, particularly for children's well-being. Drawing on the work of Ben-Arieh (2005), Fattore et al. (2018) put forward crucial questions regarding children's participation, such as the point within the research process that children should participate, and how children should be included in research on their well-being. They assert that children should be actively engaged and involved in every aspect of the research process, namely the design of the study, as participants, co-researchers (data collectors), data analysis, and dissemination. Hultgren and Johannson (2018) propose an alternative to the ladder-based models of participation. They put forward a model of participation comprising three interdependent levels: an ontological level, an ideological level, and an implementation level. The consideration and integration of 'empowering research' (Holt, 2004) is critical, as it emphasizes the processual and collaborative nature of participation. This reflects the definition of child participation put forward by the United Nations Committee on the Rights of the Child, General Comments No. 12 (2009), which focused on the 'right to be heard'.

Prior to the UNCRC, children were generally considered to lack agency and the capacity to participate in the 'adult' or public domain (Carroll et al., 2019; Lansdown, 2010). Carroll et al. (2019) note that there are continuing debates regarding children's ability to participate, and the role of their views and 'voices' in the policy sphere. The appraisal of knowledge propagated by child-led research has been delineated in terms of being 'scientific', 'practical', or 'situated research' (see Carroll et al., 2019; Hammersley, 2000) that empowers children by being involved in the decision-making dialogue and processes. There are, however, legally binding requirements to ensure and uphold the rights of each child as enshrined in the UNCRC. As indicated, Article 12 of the UNCRC advances children's right to be heard on the matters that affect them. The United Nations Committee on the Rights of the Child emphasizes the implementation of the right of the child to be heard in various settings and situations, namely:

- in the family;
- education and school activities;
- in situations of violence;
- alternative care;
- healthcare, play recreation, sports, and cultural activities;
- in the workplace;
- in the development of prevention strategies;
- in immigration and asylum proceedings;
- in emergency situations;
- and in national and international settings.

In this regard, Lundy (2007) put forward four steps that should be followed in order to attain 'Respect for the views of the child' (Article 12), namely space, voice, audience, and influence. Using these steps as a critical point of departure, Kennan et al. (2018) conducted a systematic review focusing on an evidence-base of effective practices in supporting children's participation in the child-welfare, child-protection, and alternate-care contexts. The findings identified four key processes that were effective in enhancing children's participation, namely advocacy, attendance at meetings, family welfare conferences, and recording a child's views. A limitation identified in the literature is the dearth of research on the effectiveness of various processes to afford children's perceptions to be fully considered (Kennan et al., 2018). Consequently, Carroll et al. (2019) note that despite the advancements in the field, marginalization of children in research and policy-making persists. They conducted a study exploring two projects on children's participation in Auckland, New Zealand, focusing on urban planning. The first explored a child peer research study on living in the city, and the second focused on consultation with children on the redevelopment of an urban space in Auckland. The authors concluded that the studies represent children's *genuine* participation within the public sphere, reflecting children's views, and thereby enhanced children's participatory skills (Carroll et al., 2019).

Within various countries around the world, a number of legislative advancements have been enacted to further solidify children's rights, particularly to be heard in matters that affect them. The further advancement of children's participatory rights and decision making that directly enhances children's citizenship is thus considered essential (Carroll et al., 2019). However, in many low- and middle-income contexts exorbitant levels of crime, violence, and inequality that children face impacts upon their rights in general. More specifically, there is a need for further focused research that advances the 'authentic participation' of children as a process, resulting in the veneration and acknowledgment of children's views. This should result in implementing children's views to improve policy and legislation that maintain and advocate their rights. A number of participatory studies have been conducted over the last decade that incorporates and values the voices and views of children in research on aspects affecting their lives. In South Africa, for example, recent research (see Adams & Savahl, 2015, 2017a; Adams et al., 2018; Benninger & Savahl, 2016; Savahl, 2010; Savahl et al., 2015a; September &

Savahl, 2009) exploring children's perspectives of their well-being and quality of life across various contexts have contributed to the literature on children's understandings from low- and middle-income contexts. These studies engaged children in research using a child participation framework and focused on understanding children's subjective perceptions of their well-being. Acknowledging the epistemological standpoint that children are knowledgeable experts on matters affecting their lives, Benninger and Savahl (2017a) put forward the Children's Delphi, a technique developed to engage children in the research process on aspects affecting their well-being.

Noting the importance of children's right to be heard, the United Nations Committee on the Rights of the Child (General Comments 12, 2012) summarize the basic requirements for the implementation thereof. They argue that children's participation should not only be effective and meaningful, but ethical. Further they advance that child participation processes should be:

- *transparent and informative* (the information should be age appropriate to express their views, venerating and detailing their participation);
- *voluntary* (participation should be voluntary with the express right to discontinue without consequence);
- *respectful* (those who work with children should have the requisite training and respect the child's views);
- *relevant* (the focus of any participation work should be relevant to the child, and children afforded the space to engender discussions about things important to them);
- *child-friendly* (this should be linked to children's diverse and evolving capacities);
- *inclusive* (children from marginalized groups should be included, and discrimination should be avoided, and should be culturally sensitive);
- *supported by training* (adults working with children must be appropriately trained to effectively engage children in a participatory manner—this could extend to training children in programs to promote effective participation);
- *safe and sensitive to risk* (this requires adults to ensure children are protected from violence and exploitation, with a clear child-protection strategy delineated); and finally,
- *accountable* (this includes monitoring, evaluation, and follow-up with children).

Therefore, 'Achieving meaningful opportunities for the implementation of article 12 will necessitate dismantling the legal, political, economic, social and cultural barriers that currently impede children's opportunity to be heard and their access to participation in all matters affecting them. It requires a preparedness to challenge assumptions about children's capacities, and to encourage the development of environments in which children can build and demonstrate capacities. It also requires a commitment to resources and training.' (United Nations Committee on the Rights of the Child, 2009; General Comment No. 12, p. 85).

Effective and relevant policy change therefore requires us to accurately capture and reflect children's voices and perspectives, to ultimately better the everyday lives of children. Essentially, this is linked to the notions of representation, responsibility, and the 'ethic of respect' for children's 'subjecthood' (Beier, 2018). This ethical standard extends beyond the rules of engaging with children and point to the value position that we ascribe to children and childhood. This value position is embedded in two questions:

1. Do we value children as valid members of society, and childhood as a valid feature of society?
2. Do we value children's capacity to make a valid contribution?

These questions ask us to reflect on our moral position as researchers and scientists. If we answer in the affirmative, then we are taking on the responsibility of contributing to the development of an ethical and moral discipline, and acknowledging that our current methodologies are not yet sophisticated enough to capture children's perspectives and experiences, and our current theorizations have not yet advanced to a level where we can fully understand the 'lifeworld' of children. It is thus critical that we adapt or develop new methodological and theoretical approaches.

An example is found in the Capability Approach (Sen, 2005), which highlights the role of children's capabilities to meaningfully contribute to all spheres they are involved in and that affect them (Fegter & Richter, 2014; Savahl et al., 2019). Valuing children's experiences, perspectives, and views as valid is necessary to cultivate a culture of acknowledging and respecting children's perspectives on the issues affecting them. Children should thus be engaged in decision-making in the home, at school, and in their community. However, this means that children must be aware of their rights and the implementation thereof as it dovetails with their ability to exercise that particular right (Granlund, 2013). Given children's rights as 'internationally acknowledged benchmarks', Lansdown and Karakara (2006) argue for children's right to be heard, and for children's well-being in general to be enhanced. This is particularly pertinent in countries where children are victims of abuse and crimes, to ensure appropriate measures are implemented to prevent future incidences of threats to children's safety.

2.3 Child Participation: Key Challenges

Along with the considerable focus on the operationalization of children's participation has been the engagement, critique, and revision of the various models of child participation (see Matthews, 2003; Thomas, 2007). A number of criticisms have been made of the theory, epistemological grounding, and practice of children's participation.

From a deeper epistemological perspective, Fattore et al. (2018) warn that even though children's rights in general, and participation rights in particular, have become accepted within larger social discourse, the broader meaning and implications of these rights and enactments of participation are somewhat ambiguous. Furthermore, they raise the concern that if used without due consideration of context, child participation runs the risk of being culturally insensitive and colonizing. Similarly, Harcourt and Einarsdottir (2011) note that social context and social relations are often overlooked in child participation initiatives. The concept of child participation could then be perceived as a normative construct rooted in a position of adult–child relations; which could potentially marginalize and alienate children who do not engender the 'norm'. The concerns raised by Fattore et al. (2018) could in some way be located in how early theoretical frameworks and conceptualizations of child participation were developed, without a contextual grounding in and consideration of the diversity of childhoods, children's experiences, and socio-political lifeworld's of children.

In the last decade, there has been a departure from earlier models of child participation that encompassed a hierarchical structure (Arnstein, 1969; Thomas, 2007). A comprehensive critique and consideration of child participation is evident in the work of Thomas (2007). Thomas (2007) notes that the use, interpretation, and intention of Hart's ladder was to provide a tool for conceptualizing and thinking about participation. However, his ladder has been widely used instead as a practical way of ascertaining the level of 'authenticity' of children's participation. The synthesis of literature on various models of child participation thus presents two divergent traditions in thinking; thus, those where 'power' is shared between adults and children, and those where power must be given over to children (Thomas, 2007). This is reflected in debates around participation being solely 'child-led' or 'child-led with the assistance of adults'. Skivenes and Strandbu (2006) in fact argue for a focus on *language* and *communication* as the core aspects that encompass shared social values and an 'intersubjective understanding' among individuals. The increasing focus in recent years has therefore been on the processual nature of child participation, and not merely as an outcome. Chawla (2001) noted two decades ago that child participation is contextual and influenced by age, gender, culture, political circumstances, setting, and resources available, which is still highly relevant. Therefore, the implementation of participation strategies with children should be context-specific and developed *with* children for whom programs and interventions are intended. Children's participation is thus a prerequisite for successful strategies in working with children at every level of society, as inadequate 'participatory mechanisms' foster a culture of non-participation. Theorizations of children's participation in low- and middle-income contexts therefore need to be mindful of how socio-economic conditions shape, and hinder, the degree to which children are able to participate (Moses, 2008). This points to the role that the socio-economic or income status of a country can play in the engagement and type of participatory research children are involved in. Another obstacle to child participation in low- and middle-income contexts in particular is that a large proportion of children are not easily accessible and able to participate given the constrained contexts in which they reside.

A key consideration that has been put forward in the empirical literature is whether children's participation in research brings about any demonstrable change in their lives (Thomas, 2007). A discussion about children's participation usually entails a consideration of children's agency and competency. Tobin (2019) asserts that meaningful participation results in developmental advancements across various domains, and enforces Article 6 (*Right to survival and development*) and Article 29 (*Right to education*). While the denotation of children's participation in research is contested, there is consensus among key scholars that Article 12 (*Respect for the views of the child*) cannot be viewed in isolation (Lundy, 2007; Lundy et al., 2019; Skelton, 2007). In this regard, Skelton (2010) notes that a rights-based approach is expedient, as it acknowledges the child–adult power dynamic.

2.4 Introducing the Children's Delphi

The Delphi method was initially established by Gordon and Helmer (1964) and encompasses engaging an expert panel to address forecasting issues, operating under the assumption that experts were the most likely to correctly answer questions in their fields. The original Delphi methodology was denoted as an experimental trend-predicting exercise with experts. The Delphi method has been used consistently across a wide range of disciplines as an iterative process with experts, with the ultimate goal of obtaining consensus on a particular issue. Participants are selected to provide expertise and opinions on a specific research topic, prediction, policy, or program. The five key features of the Delphi typically include anonymity, iteration, controlled feedback, statistical group response, and stability in response (Hanafin & Brooks, 2005). While the Delphi method has been utilized by researchers exploring children's quality of life, the vast majority of these studies comprised panels of adult professionals who were considered 'experts' in their respective disciplines. A gap in the Delphi literature therefore the inclusion of children as experts on their lives. This gap is ontological rather than methodological. We advocate for the use of the *Children's Delphi* to address this gap.

The Children's Delphi was initially established and piloted through a study focused on developing recommendations for intervention programs aimed at improving the self-concept and overall well-being of children residing in two urban communities in Cape Town, South Africa (see Benninger & Savahl 2017a). The overall design of the study was grounded in the principles and values of child participation, premised on the notion that children are experts of their lives and experiences. While Benninger and Savahl (2017a) used the Children's Delphi as a participatory technique to meaningfully include children in the research process, it is more than a data collection technique. Rather, it resonates with children's rights (in particular the key concept of authentic participation), theoretical and epistemological assertions encapsulated in sociological theories of childhood, and the Child Indicator Movement. The nature of the Delphi allows for its application as a stand-alone technique, as a distinct method in a multi-method study (see Adams et al., 2020), or as an overarching framework or research design for the meaningful inclusion of children's authentic perspectives.

As a stand-alone technique, the Children's Delphi can be used as a data collection technique for studies where the aims and objectives require children's subjective perceptions, knowledge, or experiences to be fairly and accurately captured and reported on. It provides a structured framework for engaging with children – ensuring depth and accuracy of interpretation. The original conceptualization of the Children's Delphi was as a distinct method in a multi-method study (see Benninger & Savahl 2017a). In this application, the researchers solicited child experts to make sense of and validate the findings of other sub-studies. Using the Children's Delphi in this manner, however, allows for more than a validation of findings; rather it advances a deeper level of interpretation. The Children's Delphi participants and the researchers worked in a collaborative capacity to unpack more nuanced meanings and interpretations. The focus was on developing an understanding and reaching consensus, with the ultimate purpose of contributing to meaningful positive change in children's lives.

As an overarching framework or research design is where the greatest potential of the Children's Delphi can be leveraged. Here the Children's Delphi should be seen as the overarching framework that guides the research process from conceptualization to dissemination, to action. There will likely be resistance to this use of the Delphi from the scientific community. For example, Adams et al. (2014) used an earlier version of the Children's Delphi in a research study on alcohol consumption and risky sexual behavior among young adults in an impoverished community in Cape Town, South Africa. The Delphi participants in this study were adolescents who were involved in the conceptualization, implementation, and dissemination phases of the study. One of the reviewers of the journal questioned the capacity of the 'child experts', claiming that the 'science' was questionable. Ironically, the Delphi participants both questioned the authenticity of the adults' responses on the questionnaires; and further argued that the standardized scales used to collect the data were not developed well enough to capture the complexity of the constructs under consideration. They essentially questioned the 'science' behind the psychometrics. This study underscores how children and young people's perspectives and input can contribute to more meaningful contextual understandings. It further points out that young people's agentic and cognitive capacities should not be considered as inherently inadequate. It highlights the value of young people collaborative capabilities and challenges the oft-accepted notion of *well-becoming*, which has a future focus fixating on adulthood. This in effect points to the postponement of the 'good life' until they reach adulthood, and implicates children and young people's right to participation and to be heard on matters affecting them, including social problems in their community and research.

Research into children's SWB has substantially advanced over the past decade. The Children's Worlds Study and the Multinational Qualitative Study on Children's Understandings of Well-Being have distilled large amounts of information on children's SWB. The discipline has moved beyond questioning the validity of the construct or the capacity of the participants (children), and there is an acknowledgment that the more relevant concern is the extent to which adults are competent enough to obtain information from children (Casas, 2016). Therefore, while advancement in psychometric instruments and innovative qualitative methods of data collection has proliferated, researchers are still hampered by the lack of first-hand insight, both at the level of theory and method. Accessing the lifeworlds of children, and understanding how they negotiate these worlds, still remains beyond the realm of contemporary scientific inquiry. It is therefore axiomatic that we partner with children to assist us to know what to ask, how to ask it, to help us interpret the information we obtain, and finally to develop strategies to transfer the data to action. The Children's Delphi provides this overarching framework (Savahl et al., 2021).

When using the Children's Delphi as a design or framework, we recommend locating the research study in children's rights and child participation discourse, and innovative theories of children and childhood. To that end, it may be useful to reconfigure Benninger and Savahl's (2017a) initial structure of the Children's Delphi as detailed below. The focus should be on the full immersion of the Children's Delphi participants into the research study, not merely into single facets of the research process, as described below.

Step 1: Selection of Children's Delphi Panel: (Purposive Sampling: Delphi participants should be specifically selected in relation to the contribution that they can make to the study. However, while it is important to ensure familiarity with the context and constructs being investigated, researchers need to ensure the fair selection of participants and that certain cohorts of children are not excluded).

Step 2: Identification of the problem (In collaboration with the Children's Delphi participants and other stakeholders).

Step 3: Identification of children's resources and skills: (Consider different languages, contextual backgrounds, and literacy levels).

Step 4: Developing capacity in researchers and Delphi participants (The researchers should be well-trained in child participation research, children's rights, and theories and methodologies related to research on children's SWB. The Children's Delphi participants should receive similar training. This is an essential step as it helps promote an effective working relationship between researchers and the Delphi participants.).

Step 5: Delphi Sessions: We recommend that the actual Children's Delphi sessions consist of a number of iterative rounds of working meetings where different phases of the research process are interrogated and executed. The Delphi participants and researchers should strive to work in a synergistic manner to ensure the authenticity of collaboration. The Delphi sessions should include the following:

- The conceptualization of the study, including the specification of the aims and objectives of the study,
- The development of data collection instruments and protocols,
- Data analysis and interpretation, and
- Enactment of dissemination and practice strategies.

2.4.1 Important Considerations: Cautionary Notes

When using the Children's Delphi, researchers should caution against perceiving the participants as a part of a reference group, who through their involvement in the project are merely required to provide a 'rubber-stamp' of validity. Another cautionary note is to ensure that the study does not adopt top-down theories of childhood, which are inconsistent with the underlying theoretical assertion of the Children's Delphi. Finally, the power relationship inherent in the research relationship needs consideration. Early commentators on child participation research (Morrow & Richards, 1996; O'Kane, 2000) noted that how to negotiate the power imbalance and create space and opportunities for children to engage in a meaningful way is ultimately the most pressing methodological challenge in childhood studies. This concern is still relevant in contemporary childhood studies.

2.5 Implications for Social Policy

Over the past 10 years, many governments around the world have made substantial advancement in the collection of objective indicators of well-being. There has also been some progress made in researching children's SWB and a steadily increasing child participation research agenda. It is well-established that both objective and subjective indicators are required in order to reach a comprehensive understanding of children's well-being (Casas & Frones, 2019; Stiglitz et al., 2009). However, it is pertinent to note that commentators lament the lack of, or the quality of available services for children, regardless of the extent to which rigorous data has been used to inform social policies or legislation. What is obfuscated, however, is a clear understanding about the point in the process at which the disjuncture is located. Is it located between data and social policy; or between social policy and service delivery? While child participation research leads to improved quality of data, the active role of children usually terminates once data collection has been completed.

The Children's Delphi provides a framework that fosters meaningful insight beyond the collection of data. The application of the Children's Delphi could assist researchers and policy-makers determine: What does the data really mean? Have the social policies developed based on this data accurately taken the data into consideration? Have the services been appropriately aligned to reflect the social policies? Are the services reaching children, and to what extent are services actually benefitting children? How can these services be improved? These are essential questions that the Children's Delphi could help address. By way of illustration, at the time of writing, the South African government as part of their commitment to the UNCRC were in the final stages of approving the fourth National Plan of Action for Children (NPAC). While the NPAC reflects a consideration of evidence-based research (using both objective indicators and children's SWB), its successful application will ultimately be contingent on the extent to which it appropriately captures the lifeworlds of children. If the process of development and enactment does not include authentic engagement with children, there is bound to be a disconnect between the data, social policy, and service delivery. To emphasize the point, for children's participation and collaboration in the research process to result in improved quality and interpretation of data, it is axiomatic that children are centrally involved in the process of policy development and service delivery strategies. Through the advancement of the Children's Delphi, we are therefore advocating for '*child-centred and informed*' policy development and service delivery. Ultimately, the application of the Children's Delphi in social policy research could prove to be an invaluable framework for contributing to the development of social policies, which reflect the authentic experiences of childhood/s, and design and deliver services that are of benefit to children and improves their overall quality of life.

For policies to be effective, we need to reach consensus on what exactly constitutes SWB, and the best ways to measure it. There also needs to be more consideration of how indicators of SWB can be integrated into the broader QoL indicator system. Recent advances in contextually relevant theoretical models and the emergence of new participatory methodologies for collecting data with children offer new possibilities. However, the stakes are high. We need to invest heavily in refining participatory methodologies; particularly, we need to sharpen our skills as it relates to engaging with and obtaining information from children (see Liebenberg et al., 2014; Theron et al., 2014). Moreover, it is recommended that the agenda for research concerning children be set by children themselves. This requires the foregrounding of children's agentic capacities and an investment by researchers to further develop these capacities. This task is particularly challenging given that children are not a homogenous group, especially in terms of their age-related cognitive capacity and cultural diversity, placing an enormous burden on researchers and practitioners in the field. The Children's Delphi offers the ideal framework to address these issues.

The greatest challenge, however, is the translation of the evidence into effective social policies. When one thinks of social policies related to children, it may be wise to think beyond traditional national policies and legislation that are often curtailed by a lack of implementation. Targeting policies at the grassroots level (e.g., municipal bylaws, school policies, etc.) to consider children's voices and ultimately the implications of their subjective perceptions and experiences would have a greater and more relevant impact on their lives.

Researchers should therefore think more broadly and target 'grassroots policies' that are more connected to the daily lives of children. The Children's Delphi provides a unique mechanism in both the translation of evidence into social policies, and the translation of social policies into effective practices and programs to improve children's lives and well-being (Savahl et al., 2019).

2.6 Conclusion

The Children's Delphi sessions are more than sites of collaboration; rather it creates the space for the intersubjective creation of meaning. It takes the notion of child participation beyond the quest for a 'valid voice' and even beyond the oft-cited gold standard of 'authentic participation'. Rather it engenders a further ontological repositioning of the subject (children and childhood), offers an option for their repositioning at the level of methodology, and turns our attention toward considering a social justice agenda for researching children's SWB.

References

Adams, S., & Savahl, S. (2015). Children's perceptions of the natural environment: A South African perspective. *Children's Geographies, 13*(2), 196–211.

Adams, S., & Savahl, S. (2017a). Children's discourses of natural spaces: Considerations for children's subjective well-being. *Child Indicators Research, 10*(2), 423–446.

Adams, S., & Savahl, S. (2017b). Nature as children's space: A systematic review. *Journal of Environmental Education, 48*(5), 291–321.

Adams, S., Savahl, S., Carels, C., Brown, Q., Malinga, M., & Zozulya, M. (2014). Alcohol consumption and risky sexual behaviour amongst young adults in a low-income community in Cape Town. *Journal of Substance Use, 19* (1–2). https://doi.org/10.3109/14659891.2012.754059.

Adams, S., Savahl, S., & Fattore, T. (2017). Children's representations of nature using photovoice and community mapping: Perspectives from South Africa. *International Journal of Qualitative Studies on Health and Well-Being*. https://doi.org/10.1080/17482631.2017.1333900.

Adams, S., Savahl, S., Florence, M., & Jackson, K. (2018). Considering the natural environment in the creation of child-friendly cities: Implications for children's subjective well-being. *Child Indicators Research, 12*(2), 545–567.

Adams, S., Savahl, S., Florence, M., Jackson, K., Manuel, D., Mpilo, M., & Isobell, D. (2020). Training emerging researchers in constrained contexts: Conducting quality of life research with children in South Africa. In G. Tonon (Ed.), *Teaching quality of life in different domains*. Springer.

Adler, A., & Seligman, M. E. P. (2016). Using wellbeing for public policy: Theory, measurement, and recommendations. *International Journal of Wellbeing, 6*(1), 1–35. https://doi.org/10.5502/ijw.v6i1.1.

Ansell, N. (2016). From objects to subjects? Children and youth in development. In J. Grugel & D. Hammett (Eds.), *The Palgrave handbook of international development* (pp. 487–511). Palgrave Macmillan UK.

Arnstein, S. (1969). Eight rungs on the ladder of citizen participation. *Journal of the American Institute of Planners, 35*(4), 216–224.

Beier, J. M. (2018). Binding gestures: A customary norm regarding the UN Convention on the Rights of the Child? *Children's Geographies*. https://doi.org/10.1080/14733285.2018.1495315

Ben-Arieh, A. (2005). Where are the children? Children's role in measuring and monitoring their well-being. *Social Indicators Research, 74*(3), 573–596.

Ben-Arieh, A. (2008). The child indicators movement: Past, present, and future. *Child Indicators Research, 1*(1), 3–16.

Benninger, E., & Savahl, S. (2016). The children's Delphi: Considerations for developing a programme for promoting children's self-concept and well-being. *Child & Family Social Work, 22*(2), 1094–1103. https://doi.org/10.1111/cfs.12329

Benninger, E., & Savahl, S. (2017a). The Children's Delphi: Considerations for developing a programme for promoting children's self-concept and well-being. *Child and Family Social Work*. https://doi.org/10.1111/cfs.12329

Benninger, E., & Savahl, S. (2017b). Children's discursive constructions of the 'self.' *Child Indicators Research, 1–29*. https://doi.org/10.1007/s12187-016-9389-8

Busseri, M. A., & Sadava, S. (2011). A review of the tripartite structure of subjective well-being: Implications for conceptualization, operationalization, analysis, and synthesis. *Personality and Social Psychology Review, 15*, 290–314.

Camfield, L., & Skevington, S. M. (2008). On subjective well-being and quality of life. *Journal of Health Psychology, 13*(6), 764–775. https://doi.org/10.1177/1359105308093860

Carroll, P., Witten, K., Asiasiga, L., & Lin, E. Y. (2019). Children's engagement as urban researchers and consultants in Aotearoa/New Zealand: Can it increase children's effective participation in urban planning? *Children and Society*. https://doi.org/10.1111/chso.12315

Casas, F. (2016). *Children participating in measuring what matters—Why, when, how?* Universal Education Foundation.

Casas, F., & Frones, I. (2019). From snapshots to complex continuity: Making sense of the multifaceted concept of child well-being. *Childhood, 27*(2), 1–15. https://doi.org/10.1177/0907568219895809

Casas, F., & Rees, G. (2015). Measures of children's subjective well-being: Analysis of the potential for cross-national comparisons. *Child Indicators Research, 8*(1), 49–69.

Chawla, L. (2001). Evaluating children's participation: Seeking areas of consensus. *PLA Notes, 42*, 9–13.

Clark, J., & S. Richards. (2017). The cherished conceits of research with children: does seeking the agentic voice of the child through participatory methods deliver what it promises?" In. I. E. Castro, M. Swauger & B. Harger (Eds.), *In Researching children and youth: Methodological issues, strategies, and innovations* (pp. 127–148). Emerald.

Cuevas-Parra, P., Stephano, M., & Zhu, Y. (2016). *Unpacking gender equality approach to children and young people's participation*. World Vision.

Diener, E. (1984). Subjective well-being. *Psychological Bulletin, 95*(3), 542–575.

Diener, E. (2009). Subjective well-being. In *The science of well-being* (pp. 11–58). Springer.

Diener, E., Suh, E. M., Lucas, R. E., & Smith, H. L. (1999). Subjective well-being: Three decades of progress. *Psychological Bulletin, 125*(2), 276–302.

Fattore, T. (2020). From object to praxis: A narrative of shifts in child well-being research. *Diskurs Kindheits- Und Jugendforschung/discourse Journal of Childhood and Adolescence Research, 15*(2–2020), 147–159. https://doi.org/10.3224/diskurs.v15i2.03

Fattore, T., Mason, J., & Watson, E. (2007). Children's conceptualisation(s) of their well-being. *Social Indicators Research, 80*, 5–29.

Fattore, T., Mason, J., & Watson, E. (2012). Locating the child centrally as subject in research: Towards a child interpretation of well-being. *Child Indicators Research, 5*, 423–435.

Fattore, T., Mason, J., & Watson, E. (2017). *Children's understandings of well-being: Towards a child standpoint*. Springer.

Fattore, T., Fegter, S., & Hunner-Kreisel, C. (2018). Children's understandings of well-being in global and local contexts: Theoretical and methodological considerations for a multinational qualitative study. *Child Indicators Research*. https://doi.org/10.1007/s12187-018-9594-8

Fegter, S. (2014). Spatial configurations of a good childhood—On the potential of praxeological approaches to research on child well-being. *Zeitschrift Fur Padagogik, 60*, 520–534.

Fegter, S., & Richter, M. (2014). Capability approach as a framework for research on children's well-being. In *Handbook of child well-being* (pp. 739–758). Springer.

Gordon, T. J., & Helmer, O. (1964). *Report on a long-range forecasting study* (No. P-2982). Rand Corporation.

Granlund, M. (2013). Participation–challenges in conceptualization, measurement and intervention. *Child Care Health Development, 39*(4), 470–473. https://doi.org/10.1111/cch.12080

Hanafin, S., & Brooks, A. M. (2005). *The Delphi technique: A methodology to support the development of a national set of child well-being indicators.* Department of child and youth affairs.
Häkli, J., & Kallio, K. P. (2018). On becoming political: The political in subjectivity. *Subjectivity, 11*, 57–73.
Hammersley, M. (2000). Varieties of social research: A typology. *International Journal of Social Research Methodology, 3*, 221–229.
Harcourt, D., & Einarsdottir, J. (2011). Introducing children's perspectives and participation in research. *European Early Childhood Education Research Journal, 19*(3), 301–307. https://doi.org/10.1080/1350293X.2011.597962
Hart, R. A. (1997). *Children's Participation: The theory and practice of involving young citizen's in community development and environmental Care.* UNESCO.
Holt, L. (2004). The 'voices' of children: De-centring empowering research relations. *Children's Geographies, 2*(1), 13–27.
Holte, A., et al. (2014). Psychology of child well-being. In A. Ben-Arieh, F. Casas, I. Frønes, & J. Korbin (Eds.), *Handbook of child well-being* (pp. 555–631). Springer.
Hultgren, F., & Johansson, B. (2018). Including babies and toddlers: A new model of participation. *Children's Geographies.* https://doi.org/10.1080/14733285.2018.1527016
Huta, V., & Ryan, R. M. (2010). Pursuing pleasure or virtue: The differential and overlapping well-being benefits of hedonic and eudaimonic motives. *Journal of Happiness Studies, 11*(6), 735–762. https://doi.org/10.1007/s10902-009-9171-4
James, A., & Prout, A. (Eds.) (1990). *Constructing and re-constructing childhood.* Falmer Press.
Kennan, D., Brady, B., & Forkan, C. (2018) Supporting children's participation in decision making: A systematic literature review exploring the effectiveness of participatory processes. *British Journal of Social Work, 48*, 1985–2002.
Langhout, R. D., & Thomas, E. (2010). Imagining participatory action research in collaboration with children: An introduction. *American Journal of Community Psychology, 46*(1–2), 60–66.
Lansdown, G. (2010). The realisation of children's participation rights: Critical reflections. In B. Percy-Smith and N. Thomas (Ed's), *A Handbook of Children and Young People's Participation: Perspectives from Theory and Practice* (pp. 11–23). Routledge.
Lansdowne, G., & Karakara, R. (2006). Children's right to express views and have them taken seriously. *Lancet, 367*, 690–692.
Liebenberg, L., Ungar, M., & Theron, L. (2014). Using video observation and photo elicitation interviews to understand obscured processes in the lives of youth resilience. *Childhood, 21*(4), 532–547. https://doi.org/10.1177/0907568213496652
Lundy, L. (2007). 'Voice' is not enough: conceptualising Article 12 of the United Nations Convention on the Rights of the Child. *British Educational Research Journal, 33*(6).
Lundy, L., Tobin, J., & Parkes, A. (2019). Article 12: The right to respect for the views of the child. In J. Tobin (2019) (Ed.), *The UN convention on the rights of the child: A commentary (Oxford Commentaries on International Law).* Oxford University Press.
Mason, J., & Watson, E. (2014). Researching children: Research on, with, and by children. In A. Ben-Arieh, F. Casas, I. Frønes, & J. E. Korbin (Eds.), *Handbook of child well-being: Theories, methods and policies in global perspective* (pp. 2757–2796). Springer.
Matthews, H. (2003). Children and regeneration: Setting an agenda for community participation and integration. *Children and Society, 17*(4), 264–276.
McKendrick, J. H. (2014). Geographies of children's well-being: In, of and for space. In A. Ben-Arieh, F. Casas, I. Frones, & J. E. Korbin (Eds.), *Handbook of child well-being: Theories, methods and policies in global perspective* (pp. 279–300). Springer.
Medvedev, O. N., & Landhuis, C. E. (2018). Exploring constructs of well-being, happiness and quality of life. *Peer J, 6*, e4903 https://doi.org/10.7717/peerj.4903
Morrow, V., & Richards, M. (1996). The ethics of social research with children: An overview. *Children in Society, 10*(2), 90–105.

Moore, K. A., Lippman, L., & Brown, B. (2004). Indicators of child well-being: The promise for positive youth development. *The Annals of the American Academy of Political and Social Science, 591*, 125–145.
Moses, S. (2008). Children and participation in South Africa: An overview. *International Journal of Children's Rights, 16*, 327–342.
O'Kane, C. (2000). The development of participatory techniques: Facilitating children's views about decisions that affect them. In P. Christensen & A. James (Eds.), *Research with children: Perspectives and practices* (pp. 136–159). Falmer.
Proctor, C., Linley, P. A., & Maltby, J. (2009). Youth life satisfaction measures: A review. *The Journal of Positive Psychology, 4*(2), 128–144.
Rye, S. A., & Vold, S. (2018). International development aid and young people's participation in societal development of the global south. *Children's Geographies*. https://doi.org/10.1080/14733285.2018.1497139
Savahl, S. (2010). *Ideological constructions of childhood*. Unpublished Doctoral Dissertation. University of the Western Cape, Bellville.
Savahl, S., Adams, S., Isaacs, S., September, R., Hendricks, G., & Noordien, Z. (2015a). Subjective well-being amongst a sample of South African children: A descriptive study. *Child Indicators Research, 8*(1), 211–226.
Savahl, S., Malcolm, C., Slembrouk, S., Adams, S., Willenberg, I. A., & September, R. (2015b). Discourses on well-being. *Child Indicators Research, 8*(4), 747–766.
Savahl, S., Adams, S., Benninger, E., Florence, M., Jackson, K., Manuel, D., Mpilo, M., Bawa, U., & Isobell, D. (2019). Researching children's subjective well-being in South Africa: Considerations for method, theory and social policy. In I. Eloff (Ed.), *Quality-of-life in African societies*. Springer.
Savahl, S., Adams, S., & Benninger, E. (2021a). The Children's Delphi: A participatory methodological framework for conducting research on children's subjective well-being in South Africa. In T. Fattore, S. Fegter, and C. Hunner-Kreisel (Hrsg.), *Children's Concepts of Well-being - Challenges in International Comparative Qualitative Research* (Chapter 9). Springer.
Savahl, S., Casas, F., & Adams, S. (2021b). The structure of children's subjective well-being. *Frontiers in Psychology. 12* (1-15).
Sen, A. K. (2005). Human rights and capabilities. *Journal of Human Development, 6*(2), 151–166.
September, R., & Savahl, S. (2009). Children's perspectives on child well-being. *Social Work Practitioner/researcher, 21*(1), 23–40.
Skelton, T. (2007). Children, young people, UNICEF and Participation. *Children's Geographies, 5*(1–2), 165–181.
Skelton, T. (2010). Taking young people as political actors seriously: Opening the borders of political geography. *Area, 42*(2), 145–151.
Skivenese, M., & Strandbu, A. (2006). A child perspective and children's participation. *Children Youth and Environments, 16*(2), 10–27.
Stiglitz J. E., Sen, A., & Fitoussi J. P. (2009). *Rapport de la Commission sur la mesure des performances économiques et du progrès social*. Ministère de l'économie, de l'industrie et de l'emploi, Présidence de la République.
Theron, L., Liebenberg, L., & Malindi, M. (2014). When schooling experiences are respectful of children's rights: A pathway to resilience. *School Psychology International, 35*(3), 253–265.
Thomas, N. (2007). Towards a theory of children's participation. *International Journal of Children's Rights, 15*, 199–218.
Tobin, J. (Ed.). (2019). *The UN convention on the rights of the child: A commentary (Oxford Commentaries on International Law)*. Oxford University Press.
United Nations Committee on the Rights of the Child (CRC). (2009). *General comment No. 12*. (2009). *The right of the child to be heard*, 20 July 2009, CRC/C/GC/12. https://www.refworld.org/docid/4ae562c52.html. Accessed 10 March 2019.
United Nations General Assembly. (1989). *Convention on the Rights of the Child*. United Nations, Treaty Series, vol. 1577, p. 3. http://www.refworld.org/docid/3ae6b38f0.html. Accessed 6 March 2016.

3 Child Participation in Nigeria: Three Examples of Dialogue with Children and Adolescents

Enrique Delamónica, Kenneth Ozoemenam, and Annie Maurice Ekanem

3.1 Introduction

This chapter documents and analyses three instances of child participation in Nigeria. A few conclusions about the nature and challenges of child participation are derived from these experiences. All three examples entail the practice of engaging with children and adolescents as part of the efforts by UNICEF to listen to their views about child poverty, understand adolescents' perspectives, and include their voices in UNICEF's work (e.g. in policy advice and in evaluation). The chapter is structured in four substantive sections and a conclusion in order to bring out the importance of listening and engaging children and adolescents. Special concerns (e.g. ethical guidelines and avoiding tokenism) peculiar to setting up dialogue mechanisms with this age group are highlighted.

Section one provides a brief overview of child participation from a generic perspective as well as introducing a particularly important previous attempt at institutionalizing child participation in Nigeria: The Nigeria Children's Parliament (NCP).

Section two summarizes an experience to elicit children's views about poverty using focus groups and other participatory methods appropriate for the respective

E. Delamónica (✉)
UNICEF, New York, USA
e-mail: edelamonica@unicef.org

K. Ozoemenam
UNICEF, Enugu, Nigeria

A. M. Ekanem
UNICEF, Port Harcourt, Nigeria
e-mail: aekanem@unicef.org

G. Tonon (ed.), *Re-defining Children's Participation in the Countries of the South*, Kindheit – Bildung – Erziehung. Philosophische Perspektiven,
https://doi.org/10.1007/978-3-662-64167-5_3

age groups (including drawings by younger children). The conflicting perspectives about poverty reduction policies is noticed. An analysis is provided of different views held by boys about the ease or difficulty girls have in coping with poverty (and vice versa).

Section three presents the results of a nation-wide qualitative review of the opinions and concerns of adolescents. This consultation was carried out in all six geopolitical zones of Nigeria. The exercise captured the voice of adolescents to find out what they think, feel, want, and expect about their situation, their role in the community, and their future. As in the previous example, participatory research tools (focus groups, problem trees, and community mapping tools) were used to gather voices of adolescents. A broad array of adolescents from various backgrounds (urban–rural, boys–girls, younger and older adolescents, different ethnic/language/religious groups, in- and out-of-school, etc.) were consulted.

Section four delves on efforts to institutionalize adolescents' voice and participation within UNICEF work and activities in Nigeria. A three-step strategy was devised. First, to practise listening to adolescents within UNICEF own programmes. Second, to periodically report adolescents' concerns and ideas within the Country Office institutional structures and evaluation efforts. Third, to transfer knowledge to national and local authorities on how to include these voices in community-level programming. In order to gain practice on meaningfully consulting children and adolescent, participation fora were carried out in half a dozen states during 2016 and 2017. In one state, the results were presented to the governor which contributed to establish a law on violence against children.

The concluding section summarizes the results and main lessons about the role of children as subjects with voice. It also points to further areas of research.

3.2 Child Participation; Conceptual Background and Previous Attempts in Nigeria

3.2.1 Conceptual Background

Children's participation and voices are important when research is about them (Ben-Arieh, 2005). Besides the well-known point that research should not be done about people without them (and their consent), the Convention on the Rights of the Child clearly indicates that children's voices need to be respected and listened to in all matters that concern them. This participation may range from individual issues, like family court proceedings, to macro ones, like nation-wide research. Although listening to children should be common sensical, it is seldom practised. This is the case in everyday life, as well as in research, in spite of the long-standing childhood research tradition (Qvortrup, 1993).

Many issues explain this deficiency, mainly misunderstanding (by adults) about, firstly, its importance and, secondly, children (even young ones) having "much to say". When engaging children and adolescents, usually participatory research methods (Chambers, 1997; Crotty, 1998; Cushing, 2015; Driskell, 2002; Groenewald, 2004; Kemmis & McTaggart, 2005; Kudva & Driskell, 2009) have been used and most of the examples in this article do so too. However, when engaging and listening to children and adolescents, it is important to do it in a proper and practical way in order to circumvent the "tyranny of participation" as "participatory" process might be liable to be used to mask power differentials, supressing (some) dissenting voices, being "pushed" by foreign donors/agendas, etc. (Cooke & Kothari, 2001).

It is also possible to learn about children's opinions using quantitative approaches. For instance, the Consensual Approach (which relies on surveys and opinion polls) has been used in both relatively richer and poorer countries, including in Africa (Gordon & Townsend, 2000; Guio et al., 2018; Mack & Lansley, 1985; Nandy & Pomati, 2015; Pomati & Nandy, 2020; Pomati et al., 2020). The utilization of qualitative and participatory techniques in the examples presented here do not arise from a belief that one method is inherently better or weaker than the other one but, rather, they are respectively more appropriate to answer some questions and address some problems.

In the type of qualitative studies described in this chapter, children's voices can be articulated orally, pictorially, theatrically, or in written form. For all of them, an ethical issue is allowing children the option of not participating (Alderson & Morrow, 2020; Berman et al., 2020; Morrow & Boyden, 2014; Powell et al., 2013; Truscott et al., 2019). There are also implementation challenges such as adapting participatory methods to age-specific cognitive capacities, abilities, and maturity of children (Iltus & Hart, 1994). This does not mean young (even very young) children cannot participate but only that their participation should be handled properly. In particular, it is important not to underrate their abilities or to minimize their views. Moreover, efforts are needed to prevent facilitators and moderators of the participatory process to influence children or to use the opportunity to impart lessons to them. Following Hart's "Participation Ladder", the best type of child participation (in the sense that it is most proactive and impactful) is when children initiate and determine its content and purpose (Hart, 1992, 2008, 2013). At the other end of the scale, the worst situation is when children are treated in a tokenistic way or as props. The examples in this article do not, unfortunately, fall into this top-level category. An issue which is addressed below.

Other practical issues range from choosing which children will participate (i.e. the issue of representation), who decides which questions to ask, what those questions will be, how many children will be participating, and where and when to meet. Group size matters to effectively carry out dialogue and exchange of ideas among children, as well as for organizing plays or asking children to prepare maps or drawings. These issues matter, for instance, for children's safety as well as making them feel comfortable to be able to express themselves and not to disrupt their lives and routines.

Representation is a particularly difficult challenge. Clearly, adults should not be choosing for them (e.g. selecting the best students in a school). However, if children oversee the selection of other children, they may also go for the best students, which will not necessarily provide the full range of voices. As with any group of humans, there is variety among children (Iltus & Hart, 1994).

3.2.2 Previous Attempts at Child Participation in Nigeria: The Children's Parliament

As part of the efforts by the Federal Government of Nigeria (FGN) to promote the rights of children to participate in decision-making processes that may be relevant to their lives and to influence decisions taken in this regard (within the family, the school, or the community), schools are supposed to provide spaces for child participation. However, not many schools, especially in semi-urban and rural areas, can afford such spaces, due, generally, to inadequate funding. Some schools do not have them at all. In urban areas, there seems to be wide disparities in this regard.

A Children's Parliament has been continuously running since the beginning of the century at the Federal level. The establishment of the Nigeria Children's Parliament (NCP), providing the opportunities given to the Nigerian children to express themselves on issues of concern to them, was established on the 14–15 December 2000. Its inception was planned and coordinated by the Child Rights Information Bureau (CRIB) of the Federal Ministry of information and National Orientation, in collaboration with UNICEF and African Children Broadcasting Network (ACBN).

One of the first activities of the NCP was to set up its organization and select different office-holders. Volunteers from a pool of about 500 children contested for President, Chief Whip, Clerk of the house, and Mace Bearer. Contestants made speeches indicating why he/she should be appointed to any of the posts being contested for and held a mock session of the parliamentary sitting. After the presentations, the children voted by a show of hands and elected the key officers of the Children's Parliament.

The President of the NCP, at the end of the first session, made two special requests and implored the Minister of Information and National Orientation to convey the same to the President of the Federation. These were:

- A media dialogue with the President of the Federal Republic of Nigeria to allow children express their views to the government and the people of Nigeria.
- The establishment of Children's parliament in every state of the Federation, including Abuja, to allow for effective participation by children on issues of concern to them.

Throughout the years, the NCP has been involved in several initiatives related to the promotion of child rights. The most important one was, perhaps, advocating for the passage of the Child Rights Act. During a period of over a decade, various stakeholders, at individual and organizational levels, had advocated for a Child Rights Act. The issue gradually became a major national debate at all levels along with strong media pressure. The President of the NCP presented 'Voices of Nigerian 'Children', a paper on the children's perspective on the proposed Child Rights Act. The president appealed that the Act be passed into Law without further delay. He also appealed for the establishment of a Children's Commission as a body to see to all the fundamentals of children developmental issues. The presentation evoked a promise from the Deputy Speaker of the House of Representatives stating that the Bill would be passed into law. The bill was passed in May 2003 by the Senate and the House of Representatives, and the President of the Federation assented to it a few months later.

The NCP has come a long way. It is now entrenched in all 36 states of the Federation and in the Federal Capital Territory. With a fixed 3-year term, membership of NCP involves a democratic process that identifies children representatives at the local government council level and, subsequently, these children contest for the electable positions at the State-level Parliament. By the third stage, successful members of State Children's Parliament contest for the two available slots (one girl, one boy) to represent their state at the national level.

Child participation is now beginning to gain some recognition by the government of Nigeria. Having recognized the NCP as a useful tool for promoting and entrenching child participation rights, the government of Nigeria now systematically calls upon the children to present their views on issues that concern them via their representatives in the NCP.

However, the situation of the NCP started to deteriorate across the country since the withdrawal of UNICEF support. A few states have managed to sustain the tempo and continued to fund the activities. Unfortunately, many other states appear to have ignored the NCP and other forms of child participation initiatives.

3.3 Children's Views About Poverty[1]

3.3.1 Background and Methodological Considerations

To educe children's views about poverty, a total of 120 children were engaged in a participatory research project. Forty children from each of three local government councils (Asari-Toru, Eleme, and Okrika) in Rivers State (Southern Nigeria) were selected. The number of children and adolescents was chosen for ease of manageability of plenary sessions. Children were randomly selected across Basic Education classes from randomly selected schools. Teachers and government staff from the State Ministry of Education assisted in this process. The random selection process was used to avoid adults (or children) selecting participants. This could have resulted in the most articulate or most popular or other salient characteristics to have been chosen. Although such a small sample in a participatory research setting is not intended to be a representative sample of all children in

[1] This section summarizes arguments which can be found in Ozoemenam et al. (2021).

Nigeria, it is still essential to ensure a wide range of voices of children (not a pre-selected one, either by adults or children, based on criteria that may "silence" some groups). Although the results reported below should not be generalized for the whole country, children provided fascinating insights about how they understand and experience poverty.

The study relied on Focused Group Discussions (FGDs) and open, unstructured questions during break-out sessions to obtain responses from the children. The questions were used to engage children aged between 7–16 years of age (unfortunately, 17-year-old adolescents were not available because they were preparing for exams). Responses were obtained in plenary, in break-out groups, and on one-on-one basis. The children had opportunity to express their views both in writing and with sketches and drawings.

Each participating school had a group of teachers that escorted the children to the meeting location. Representatives of Rivers State Universal Basic Education Board, the Ministry of Budget and Economic Planning, and the Ministry of Social Welfare were all in attendance to support the process. While the state government led the process as host of the meeting, UNICEF provided technical guidance and support to a group of facilitators pre-trained to moderate some segments of the exercise.

No lectures or presentations about poverty, child poverty or related matters were made before the FGDs and interviews with children; only brief instructions and ground rules for the various exercises. Also, a modestly suitable physical and psychological environment was created that encouraged the free expression of thoughts and ideas by the children. Most importantly, all participating children received assurances that there will be no repercussions for communicating their views during the session.

3.3.2 Children's Understanding of Poverty

According to the children, poverty is about the capacity (or lack of it) to acquire or access necessities of life. This includes shelter, food, and clothing. Families that do not have these necessities or who struggle to provide these necessities are considered poor. Thus, according to the children, poverty can be determined by the type and quality of material goods or physical assets they possess. While the rich person can live in a properly secured house, own cars, and use modern electronics, the poor cannot enjoy similar comfort. Expressed in free-hand drawings, the children noted that the poor would usually live in houses built with mud and thatched roofs, while the rich live in houses built with blocks and zinc roofs or more modern roofing sheets. Other expressions of poverty included people who were destitute or begged on the streets.

Physical appearances and attributes play a crucial role in identifying the rich from the poor. Ironed and clean uniform, kempt hair, shoes, books, school bag, and writing materials were used to denote a child from a rich home. These children were depicted as well-fed, properly clothed in attractive school uniforms, alighting from flashy cars on arrival at school, carrying well-stocked lunch boxes. The converse side of this scenario was used to describe a child from a poor home. The drawings depicted children from poor families trekking to school barefoot, frequently on an empty stomach, clad in tattered school uniforms, with worn school bags/boxes, containing a few or even no books at all.

In addition, children observed that society treats the poor with contempt, excluding them from access to necessities of life and from social interactions with people of higher socio-economic status. Such exclusion, they argued, could result in a negative psychological impact on poor children, hindering them from realizing their fullest potentials. In their view, negative sentiments of jealousy and malice are also likely to develop in the minds of the poor, particularly when affluence is frequently displayed around them.

3.3.3 Effects of Poverty on Children

In keeping with their understanding of poverty, the children opined that poverty affects them when their parents are poor and unable to cater to their basic needs. Some of those needs include, for instance, school fees, books, writing materials, food, shoes, or adequate clothing.

The children unanimously agreed that peer pressure was a real and inevitable challenge for many poor children, given its potential to lure young people into prostitution, armed robbery, and delinquency. The connection between poverty and risks (e.g. of violence) was pervasive among children.

Hawking was also seen as an effect of poverty on children because it required them to work to supplement the family's income. Interestingly, however, there were somewhat conflicting views (or rather feelings) about this. While children acknowledged that it was unacceptable for children to work, they also said that sometimes it was necessary, if the family's living condition required that children hawk to support the home. Some of these conditions included the need to generate additional savings for the family, provide food, and help out an ailing parent; others include contribution towards payment of the house rent and school fees and personal upkeep. Nevertheless, it was generally observed that this condition exposed both girls and boys to violence, exploitation, and abuse. They also included dropping out of school for both girls and boys as another result of poverty.

When asked if poverty affects boys and girls similarly or differently, two contrasting perspectives arose. While some agreed that poverty affects boys and girls differently, others argued that it was the same for boys and girls from the same home.

More interestingly, some boys argued that boys suffered more because they were naturally predisposed to engaging in hard labour. But the very narrow range of available work options remain a considerable challenge to the boy-child who must engage in long-term labour in order to escape poverty. Whereas girls, they said, could get married, engage in simple vocational activities, and thus escape poverty.

In contrast, many girls claimed boys have it easier than girls. They highlighted that girls end up as domestic servants or be pressured into getting married or into prostitution while boys continue their education. Some of them also identified other consequences, such as teenage pregnancy (although illegal in Nigeria, children also mentioned the existence of abortion and they were aware of the health risks for girls).

3.3.4 Solutions to Poverty

The children recommended three possible approaches to addressing poverty. Social welfare by the government featured highly on the list of recommendations. They said that it was the sole responsibility of government to provide employment and subsidize the cost of basic goods for the poor. However, there was also a strong case for the opposite view that individuals should take ownership of their poverty status and engage in meaningful activities that would yield desired results. Acquiring vocational skills is one way through which people could begin the process of escaping poverty. The children also advised that there was strength in forming cooperative societies and associations at the community level to harness poverty alleviation efforts. Focusing only on government's subsidy was, for them, not a sustainable way to address poverty in the community or at household levels.

3.4 Voice of Adolescents: Listening to What They Think, Feel, Want, and Expect

The results of this section emerge mainly from a collaboration with Action Aid Nigeria. Students from various universities throughout the country participated as facilitators and moderators of the activities with children and adolescents. A qualitative review of the opinions and concerns of adolescents was carried out to capture the (diverse) voices of adolescents and to find out what they think, feel, want, and expect about their situation, their role in the community, and their future. Different participatory appraisal tools were used to gather the voices of a variety of children and adolescents.

3.4.1 Preliminaries

Methods: Focus Group Discussion (FGD) was used as the primary tool to collect information. Other participatory tools such as vulnerability mapping, activity profiles, problem tree and solution tree were applied too. The research instruments were respondent-group specific. The instruments were designed to be open-ended and included probes for potential additional issues that could emerge as important concerns among the adolescents. All the instruments were designed in English. Though no translations were made, enumerators for the research were drawn from the localities to help with local interpretation of the questions when and where it became necessary.

Target Population and Study Locations: There were four intersecting categories of respondents: in-school and out-of-school, girls and boys, within the age range of 10–14 and 15–19, and urban/rural/peri-urban that were considered to participate in the FGDs. In each of the seven locations, all the combinations of these four groups were represented.

There are 36 states in Nigeria, in addition to the Federal Capital Territory, divided into 774 Local Government Areas (LGAs). States are also grouped into six geopolitical zones, which have no legal or administrative status. However, they carry political and identity weight and importance. For a balanced distribution of research sites, locations were chosen from one state per geopolitical zone, and also from the Federal Capital. The selected states were:

- Akwa Ibom (south–south)
- Adamawa (north-east)
- Benue (north-central)
- Abuja (Federal Capital Territory, FCT)
- Imo (south-east)
- Kano (north-west)
- Lagos (south-west).

All states are divided into several Local Government Areas and grouped into three senatorial districts. An average of eighteen FGDs held in each of the three senatorial districts of these states. Within these senatorial districts, locations were chosen from LGAs covering Urban, Semi-Urban, and Rural areas.

Data Collection: The FDGs and other activities were carried out in May of 2015. On average, each FGD took about an hour. In all the schools, children and adolescents were enthusiastic about participating. There were some challenges finding out-of-school children in the south-east part of the country, where school enrolment is above the national average. In such cases, the Key Informant Interview (KII) technique was used with the informed consent of the participants. The distribution of the over 1,300 participating children and adolescents is described in Table 3.1.

3.4.2 The Situation of the Adolescents

Children or adolescents or young adults? Most in-school adolescents 10–14 (girls and boys) in urban, semi-urban, and rural areas responded they were children ("We are children because we are still under our parents who are responsible for our needs"). While most out-of-school 10–14 and 15–19 adolescents (girls or boys) see themselves as young adults ("because we fend for ourselves"); some describe

Table 3.1 Distribution of participating children and adolescents by state

Adamawa	Categories	Girls	Boys	Total
	In-school (10–14 years)	60	45	**105**
	In-school (15–19 years)	32	25	**57**
	Out-of-school (10–14 years)	11	11	**22**
	Out-of-school (15–19 years)	66	39	**105**
	Adamawa total	**169**	**120**	**289**
Akwa Ibom	In-school (10–14 years)	33	42	**75**
	In-school (15–19 years)	30	44	**74**
	Out-of-school (10–14 years)	01	01	**02**
	Out-of-school (15–19 years)	05	01	**06**
	Akwa Ibom total	**69**	**88**	**157**
Benue	In-school (10–14 years)	31	33	**64**
	In-school (15–19 years)	29	29	**58**
	Out-of-school (10–14 years)	0	0	**0**
	Out-of-school (15–19 years)	19	30	**49**
	Benue total	**79**	**92**	**171**
Federal Capital Territory	In-school (10–14 years)	30	30	**60**
	In-school (15–19 years)	20	33	**53**
	Out-of-school (10–14 years)	07	06	**13**
	Out-of-school (15–19 years)	16	13	**29**
	Federal Capital Territory total	**73**	**82**	**155**
Imo	In-school (10–14 years)	51	50	**101**
	In-school (15–19 years)	58	51	**109**
	Out-of-school (10–14 years)	0	1	**1**
	Out-of-school (15–19 years)	0	0	**0**
	Imo total	**109**	**102**	**211**
Kano	In-school (10–14 years)	48	46	**94**
	In-school (15–19 years)	23	34	**57**
	Out-of-school (10–14 years)	12	0	**12**
	Out-of-school (15–19 years)	24	20	**44**
	Kano total	**107**	**100**	**207**
Lagos	In-school (10–14 years)	51	37	**88**
	In-school (15–19 years)	20	30	**50**
	Out-of-school (10–14 years)	09	0	**09**
	Out-of-school (15–19 years)	07	26	**33**
	Lagos total	**87**	**93**	**180**

(continued)

Table 3.1 (continued)

Adamawa	Categories	Girls	Boys	Total
Nation-wide	***Grand Total***	*693*	*677*	*1370*

Source: internal documentation provided by Action Aid to UNICEF Nigeria Country Office

themselves as children because "people still look after us even in our situation". Some of them are apprentices, and others living in camps as internally displaced persons (IDPs). Other expressions children in these situations used were: "we are most times on our own"; "and our families care little about us"; "we are also labelled as fools because we are not in school".

Many of the respondents hinted at undertones of rivalry regarding their peers. Still, some others spoke of their peers with some great sense of respect and solidarity. Others also mentioned the threat of negative peer influence, pressuring them to do things they would not want to do.

Regarding adults, adolescents admire adults for their independence and maturity and would want to be like them ("We see some adults as parents and role models because they always see the best in us. We also see them as individuals with greater freedom, and they go places where they want to go without restrictions"). However, there are areas of concern in terms of academic pressure, insufficient recognition for their efforts ("I see adults as our guardians, but they sometimes expect so much from us, they don't see the good we have done from childhood. They are so mindful of academic success they forget the progress we have made"), and the realization of hypocrisy in the way adults behave ("Many adults are hypocrites. They tell us one thing and do another and think that we don't know but we know"). Clearly, children do not feel and think about all adults the same. The admiration (or even disappointment) they feel about their parents is very different from their perception of other adults, in particular authority figures ("We have harsh teachers though some of them are kind"; "Police see us as thieves and we see them as even bigger thieves").

In terms of their activities, children use some of their time reading or doing assignments. Some girls also mention they chat or lie-down, play indoor games, or make some food to sell to raise some money. The adolescent boys, regardless of age, say they play soccer, visit friends, chat or watch television, play video games, browse the internet, read newspapers or magazines, etc. The out-of-school children say they use free moments or leisure hours to relax or socialize. Otherwise, they spend most of their time doing something useful to earn some money.

Gender

The topic of activities and time-use highlighted existing gender differences. The description of gender-differentiated activities performed (or made to perform, due to socially prevailing normative expectations) by boys and girls were similar, despite the geographic locations of the girls or boys describing them: "There are boy's work and a girl's work". "A girl's work is to wash clothes, and cook while the boys fetch water". Nevertheless, both boys and girls mentioned dissatisfaction about this state of affairs. Boys claimed that girls are given less labour-intensive tasks at school and at home: "Girls cook and bath young ones; boys fetch firewood". On the other hand, girls claimed that boys do not perform as many duties or go on errands as much as them: "Girls are trained to cook, sweep and arrange the house etc., but the boys are not taught to do so, and I become angry when they mess up where I have cleaned". Girls mentioned that the boys are allowed much more freedom to express themselves. One specific response was common across states: "Boys don't cook or clean their rooms at home, and their parents allow them to go out and come back any time they like". The girls also mentioned that they are not taken as seriously as the boys. However, boys argued that they are given more strenuous tasks like chopping wood and cutting grass in school. In addition, boys claimed that the girls are not treated with as much severity as they are when it comes to punishments: "Even in school the boys are given harder punishments than the girls".

These responses suggest how culture and society influence gender opportunities, challenges, and constrains (and the children's views about them). Some boys agreed, saying: "Boys are given more money than the girls. Boys are more respected. Girls are not taken seriously because they will end up at a husband's house". "Honestly girls are given more priority than we boys at home and in the school because they require special attention. We, boys, are at liberty to a lot of things but girls are restricted for security purposes". The girls' voices clearly suggest bitterness regarding the ways and manner they (girls) are treated at home and in school ("I do all the work in the house while my brother plays and watches football"). They cannot express themselves because they do not enjoy the same freedom as the boys in the home.

Adolescents Roles: Family, Schools, and Community

In the Family: The responses across the states did not show an impressive level and quality participation of adolescents in what happens in their families. Some adolescents mentioned that they are consulted but most times their views are not considered. Particularly, the 10–14 adolescent girls and boys responded that they are hardly considered or consulted. However, the 15–19 female and male adolescents said they are involved even though most times their contributions are minimal.

Across the states, the average adolescent functions in the family by helping in menial tasks and chores. This response reflects across all the urban, semi-urban, and rural communities. The difference in the social and culture contexts of the different contexts notwithstanding, the overall picture deriving from the activity profiles suggest that adolescents are doing so much in their families. Most adolescents begin their day quite early. The activity profiles indicate that adolescents wake up by 5.00 a.m. and some by 4.30 a.m. daily. These include Saturdays and Sundays. Adolescents indicate that they wake up early to carry out domestic chores both before and after school. Some of their responsibilities are:

- Sweeping the compound
- Fetching water
- Washing parents/guardians' car

- Preparing younger siblings for school
- Washing plates/Cleaning the kitchen
- Preparing meals
- Assisting mothers to prepare foodstuff for sale
- Supporting parents in the market or farms
- Running errands
- Grind corn, millet, etc.
- Wash parents/guardians/siblings' clothes or uniforms
- Hawking.

The out-of-school adolescents across the states have similar narratives. It is a different experience, however, for the adolescents in IDPs Camps. Some of them wake up from 6.00am to clean up and prepare for school. Adolescents not going to school in the Camp wake up much later. After school, "we go to the kitchen to collect food, eat, read and relax". However, some of them also had other concerns specific to their situation. They expressed them as: "We want to go home", "we want to complete secondary school education"; "In this environment, we cannot achieve our hopes and dreams".

In the Community: Similarly to the way they feel about their family involvement, adolescents say their influence on what happens in the community is marginal. Many of the respondents in and out-of-school said they are called to join in the community cleaning and organizing. Out-of-school adolescents say they are involved in youth clubs and minor vigilante groups. Adolescent girls seem to be tasked with provision of some basic services like water and food when activities are been carried out. Also, adolescents are involved with religious activities like in the church or mosque. The main roles of adolescents are:

- Running errands for the elder members of the community
- Obeying basic rules of the community
- Rendering services for the elderly in the community, if needed, e.g. helping them cross streets, fetching water for them, or assisting them to carry heavy loads, etc.
- Participate during environmental sanitation or recreational activities, i.e. filling of potholes on the roads, clearing of bushes around public spaces and helping with the arrangement of venues during social events in the community.
- Helping with the clearing and cleaning of worship places
- Assisting in religious lessons.

In many states, the role of the adolescent girls' in the community is limited to domestic chores (echoing the gender differences mentioned earlier). They are not involved with community chores except where there is a special activity involving every community member, especially during construction of worship places. The in-school girls aged 15–19 in Imo state commented thus: "We are involved sometimes in the family; we are not involved in the community" and "Yes, girls are discriminated against when it comes to doing chores."

The out-of-school children and adolescents contribute in their respective communities too. They are involved with the general sanitation of the community. They sometimes act as security guards. Also, they assist the aged persons who do not have or whose children are not around to perform basic chores and run errands for them.

It would appear not many schools, especially in semi-urban and rural areas, encourage spaces for child participation. Some schools do not offer them at all. The responses from the urban areas showed a remarkable difference in this regard. Nonetheless, the responses revealed the existence of some associations and clubs in their respective schools and communities but no active involvement in the school per se. Extra-curricular activities seem to be as far as the horizon of "school participation" reaches (for children, adolescents, and adults).

Their Future

Wishes: The in-school and out-of-school adolescents, rural or urban, have great expectations. Most in-school children desire to become successful persons in life, independent and responsible citizens. Every adolescent girl expressed a desire to further her education to the tertiary level and emerge as a professional in the future. Most boys expressed the same aspirations, but some said they would like to be successful businessmen. They hope to achieve these goals through the different professions they aspire to become. Interestingly, it is hard to notice much of a difference in aspirations and dreams between boys and girls (other than, perhaps, the type of careers they expect would be open to them).

Worries: Their hopes and dreams notwithstanding, adolescents have huge worries. Though some of the worries expressed generally apply to all the categories, some are peculiar with specific groups. One predominant remark from the in-school girls and boys that apply to rural, semi-urban, and urban locations is the worry about "the poor learning facilities and infrastructure in their schools". Most in-school adolescents visibly expressed worry about the poor nature of their classrooms, libraries, laboratories, hostels, and their teachers. They are worried that their teachers are not adequately remunerated and their performance in school will drop, and their hopes may not be achieved: "I worry that we don't have good school facilities and our laboratory is not well equipped; that we need trained teachers to transfer good knowledge to us.". Another aspect of uncertainty for many students is about doing well in exams, finishing school, and being able to find jobs when they grow up: "I worry about my studies: if I don't study I will not be what I want to be in the future"; "I fear lack of finances to further my education"; "I fear unemployment after graduation".

The in-school children also worry about the regular increase in school fees. The persistent increase can cause poor students to drop out of school. Some are not particularly happy with their living condition. The environment they live in does not allow them to concentrate even after school. Adolescents also worry about the lack of a steady supply of electricity. Many in-school children are unable to read at night as a result. Some girls worry about the possibility of continuing with their education, reiterating the gender dynamic mentioned above. As they said: "our parents will not accept because our parents feel and believe that girls who are allowed to continue their education get 'spoiled'".

In-school adolescents also worry about insecurity in their communities and schools; high crime rate in their areas; bad roads; excessively overworked with domestic chores; and too many assignments. They also mentioned worrying about peer pressure. Children also expressed concerns and fears related to death (their own or their parents): "Fear of death, that I might not accomplish my dream because of insurgency".

Challenges: It is important to mention that the challenges of in-school children in rural, semi-urban, and urban are significantly different from the challenges confronting out-of-school adolescents and those among IDPs. Whereas in-school, urban adolescents' challenges centre on the lack of subject teachers, high school fees, lack of qualified teachers, peer pressure, poor infrastructure in schools, poor results, lack of access to internet and water, or scant future job opportunities, out-of-school adolescents and those among IDPs face the challenges of food and human security.

Moreover, the out-of-school rural, semi-urban, and urban consider poverty and poor guidance from parents and adults, peer pressure, rape, ritual killings, sexual harassment, discrimination by society, joblessness, and lack of vocational training opportunities, among others as their challenges. The challenges of adolescents in difficult circumstances are equally informed by their current conditions. Lack of proper feeding in the camps, bullying, fear of attacks, unplanned marriage, drug abuse, homelessness, lack of attention from parents, emotional challenges due to missing parents, and poor living and health conditions.

For adolescents among IDPs, the insurgency (which made them move from their original dwellings and location), lack of education, and poor and inadequate feeding in the camp were the highest-ranked challenges.

The problem tree analysis and the vulnerability maps have shown how adolescents perceive and understand their environments. Vulnerability maps illustrated accident-prone areas, places perceived to be unsafe for young people, especially girls, school, and community areas where peers hang out and engage in lawless acts.

As in other topics, the challenges take a gendered turn. Girls expressed them in terms of sexual harassment and unplanned pregnancy as key challenges. Also, some girls mentioned, "finding a good husband" as a future challenge.

3.5 Institutionalizing Adolescents' Voice and Participation in UNICEF Nigeria

Based on the results mentioned in the previous section, the UNICEF Country Office in Nigeria concluded that it is imperative to institutionalize adolescents' voice and participation. To provide space for adolescent participation and learn how to regularly consult meaningfully with them, several adolescent participation fora were carried out in the North-Western states of Kaduna, Kano, Katsina, and Rivers State in Southern Nigeria during 2017.

A three-step strategy was devised. First, to practise listening to adolescents within UNICEF own programmes. Second, to periodically report adolescents' concerns and ideas within the institutional structures of the country office. Third, once this is achieved (it was expected to take a few years), use the documented evidence of the benefits of listening to adolescents to transfer knowledge on how to include these voices in state-level programming and policy-making by the government.

The selection of children and adolescents was like the one described in the previous section. For example, a total of 42 adolescents between the ages of 12–19 were consulted in Daudawa settlement (Katsina). There were slightly fewer girls than boys (19 and 23, respectively). In total, three-quarters of them were attending school. There were five married girls among the consulted adolescents. Of the 33 adolescents who participated in the Birnin Kuka settlement assessment (Katsina), 16 were girls. Almost three-quarters of all the participants were attending school.

3.5.1 Water Services and Infrastructure

Providing context to their access to social goods and services within their communities, the adolescents opined that water was supplied through solar and handheld water pumps. They, however, expressed a preference for solar water because it is powered via sunlight, which is always available, easy to fetch, and tastes better. Further inquiries about their knowledge on water and sanitation provided insight into some of their expectations which were the need to eradicate open defecation, make water safe for drinking, and provide adequate water, sanitation and hygiene (WASH) facilities in schools, especially for the girls. To further bolster the importance of accessing clean drinking water, they identified contaminated water as a source of some adolescents' illnesses.

Furthermore, the adolescents listed other infrastructure needs in the community. They mentioned: a good access road into the town, a market, a modern hospital, and renovated classrooms, which were noted to be dilapidated, as some of the key expectations for their communities.

3.5.2 Education and Schools

As expressed in terms of the opportunities it presents, the role education plays in the lives of the children was explored. Some of the reasons proffered included a chance to bond with a classmate during in-class sessions, free period (which is used for jesting or chatting), or during early morning assembly gatherings; learning about new subjects like hygiene, how to respect one's elders, and acquiring knowledge which could translate into helping their parents in the future. One of the girls mentioned that she liked school because it had afforded her a leadership position (i.e. school captain), which made her peers' envy.

Some frustrations with the school system included the absence of teachers during school hours; the inability of other children to attend school because their parents' could not provide basic school needs; rough play during recreational periods; punishments for lateness due to domestic chores which had to be attended to before going to school; fear of corporal punishment and continuous recitation of Islamic verses. The students were also able to identify (and consequently like) teachers who understood well their subjects and who had an engaging and clear teaching style from those who did not.

The best-liked teachers at school were those teaching mathematics, English, agriculture, computer, biology, and economics. The adolescents were drawn to these subjects because they were their favourite (i.e. agriculture); delivered using a methodology which aided their understanding (i.e. biology, economics, and mathematics); provided new knowledge for their daily use/practice (e.g. English); and was popularly modelled by others and thus presented an opportunity for their inclusiveness (i.e. computer).

Specific school days were also liked for the following reasons:

a) Monday, we all become so clean (our uniforms are washed, fingers and hairs cut)
b) Wednesday, it's termed as Labour Day (we keep the school and its environs clean)
c) Friday, school closes on time. We get an opportunity to attend to sports and exercise.

In addition to these reviews about schooling/education, the adolescents acknowledged challenges faced by some of their peers and the reasons for not attending school. The children made the distinction between actively and regularly going to school or not. Thus, not attending school is differentiated from skipping a school day which, according to the children, could be due to staying at home to play or not having finished homework to be presented in class. These constraints for not attending school (regularly and consistently) include lack of adequate nutrition (which could interfere with timely attendance at school); engaging in domestic chores during school hours; lack of commitment by uneducated parents who are not interested and engaged in their children's education, and mingling with bad friends.

3.5.3 Violence Against Children

In Katsina, the results of some of the consultations were presented to the governor. This helped to make progress towards establishing a law on violence against children and domestication of the Child Rights Act, which was finally passed into law a couple of years later. The Child Rights Act is not just about violence but includes other aspects (like the right to health and education). The evidence and voices about the difficulties children faced with lack water and attending school (related to fees, weakness due hunger, and problems with teachers) were also instrumental to lobby for the state-level Child Rights Act.

Before starting the conversations with children, it had been agreed that questions about violence were not going to be asked. The reasons for this were ethical ones. If a child had been subject to violence, there might be an obligation on the part of facilitators to refer the issue to the police or the justice system. Also, the facilitators were not trained to be able to offer psychological counselling to the child. In any case, at that time Nigeria was a pathfinder country in the campaign to End Violence Against Children. An extensive survey had just been completed (National Population Commission et al., 2016). It provided the quantitative evidence required to design policies and programmes against the various types of violence (physical, sexual, and emotional). Thus, there was no need to address violence against children in these dialogues.

Nevertheless, sometimes, albeit not in personal terms, children would bring up specific issues related to violence and abuse. One of them (which was also present in the previous section's consultations) was violent school discipline. Another was intra-family conflicts and fighting. The third one was the issue of street and neighbourhood safety.

3.6 Conclusion: Limitations, Further Work, Research Prospects

Several lessons can be summarized from these three examples. Some are substantive, while other ones relate to processes and practices.

Among the former, although the results of consultations with children and adolescents were much more extensive and richer than what is summarized here, two generic conclusions stand out. Admitting it was known beforehand, one of them was the pervasiveness of gender differences. Nevertheless, it is important to listen to this message directly from children (and how they express it). The second one is children's concerns about their lack of voice—in their families, at school, within their communities. In addition, at a more specific level, children have clarity about the context in which they live, such as, for instance, the risks they face and the areas which are not safe in their communities, the conditions and consequences of child poverty, the quality of their school buildings and teachers' ability to teach.

The dialogue with children made it palpable that they can provide information for UNICEF programmes. They have knowledge about what is working (or not in their communities). This information could be used to design better programming and policies and contribute to public advocacy and, eventually, to influence policy.

This, of course, requires paying attention to the practicalities of the processes to incorporate children's voices. Turning to practice issues, the most important conclusion from these examples is that it is possible to listen to children (even in the context of little child participation/voice). Moreover, this can be done in various (complementary) ways. One of them is going to where the children live, which is more ethical and practical than bringing a "representative" child to a (possibly intimidating and certainly boring, unappealing) adult context to "speak" for children. Another is to organizing state- and country-wide representative groups of (diverse) children through their self-selection (as it is done with the Nigeria Children's Parliament). In both of these, and other endeavours to listen to children, it is crucial to avoid tokenism.

However, there are limitations, even in these successful examples. One of them (following Hart's ladder) is that adults initiated all the examples described here. These are not good experiences of child-initiated processes. Also, these experiences are not institutionalized yet. Some of them were not properly followed up when external support was withdrawn (putting into question their sustainability). Also, there are no set time and space at senior or mid-level management meetings to periodically incorporate the lessons of listening to children. Moreover, no feedback loops to the children and their communities have been established (yet!).

Some of these limitations can be overcome with further practice and continuing these experiences through time. In so doing, and thinking of further research to better understand these processes, more questions regarding power (and its expression at the local level) and how it hinders children's and adolescents' voices and participation. Additionally, more research about the limitations of these approaches is also needed. A good source to start exploring and asking questions about these topics is... children themselves.

References

Alderson, P., & Morrow, V. (2020). *The ethics of research with children and young people: A practical handbook*. Sage.

Ben-Arieh, A. (2005). Where are the children? Children's role in measuring and monitoring their well-being. *Social Indicators Research, 74*, 573–596. https://doi.org/10.1007/s11205-004-4645-6.

Berman, G., K., Carter, M., Herranz, G., & Sekara, V. (2020). Digital contact tracing and surveillance during COVID-19. General and child-specific ethical issues, *Innocenti Working Papers no. 2020–01*, UNICEF Office of Research – Innocenti, Florence.

Chambers, R. (1997). *Whose reality counts: Putting the first last*. Intermediate Technology Publications Ltd (ITP).

Cooke, B., & Kothari, U. (Eds.). (2001). *Participation: The New Tyranny?* Zed Books.

Crotty, M. (1998). *The foundations of social research: Meaning and perspective in the research process*. Sage.

Cushing, D. F. (2015). Promoting youth participation in communities through youth master planning. *Community Development, 46*(1), 43–55. https://doi.org/10.1080/15575330.2014.975139.

Driskell, D. (2002). *Creating better cities with children and youth: A manual for participation*. UNESCO and Earthscan.

Gordon, D., & Townsend, P. (2000). *Breadline Europe: The measurement of poverty*. Policy Press.

Groenewald, T. (2004). A phenomenological research design illustrated. *International Journal of Qualitative Methods, 3*(1), 42–55. https://doi.org/10.1177/160940690400300104.

Guio, A., Gordon, D., Marlier, E., Najera, H., & Pomati, M. (2018). Towards an EU measure of child deprivation. *Child Indicators Research, 11*, 835–860. https://doi.org/10.1007/s12187-017-9491-6.

Hart, R. (1992). Children's participation: From Tokenism to Citizenship. *UNICEF Innocenti Essays, No. 4*. International Child Development Centre of UNICEF.

Hart R. (2008). Stepping back from 'The Ladder': Reflections on a model of participatory work with children. In: A. Reid, B. B. Jensen, J. Nikel, & V. Simovska (eds.) *Participation and learning*. Springer.

Hart, R. (2013). *Children's participation: The theory and practice of involving young citizens in community development and environmental care.* UNICEF and Earthscan.

Iltus, S., & Hart, R. (1994). Participatory planning and design of recreational spaces with children. *Architecture & Comportement/architecture & Behaviour, 10*(4), 361–370.

Kemmis, S., & McTaggart, R. (2005). Participatory action research: Communicative action and the public sphere. In N. K. Denzin & Y. S. Lincoln (eds.), *The Sage handbook of qualitative research* (pp. 559–603). Sage.

Kudva, N., & Driskell, D. (2009). Creating space for participation: The role of organizational practice in structuring youth participation. *Community Development, 40*(4), 367–380. https://doi.org/10.1080/15575330903279705.

Mack, J., & Lansley, S. (1985). *Poor Britain.* George Allen & Unwin.

Morrow, V., & Boyden, J. (2014). Ethics of Researching Children's Well-Being. In A. Ben-Arieh, F. Casas, I. Frønes, & E. J. Korbin (eds.), *Handbook of child well-being: Theories, methods and policies in global perspective* (pp. 2895–2918). Springer Netherlands.

National Population Commission of Nigeria, UNICEF Nigeria, and the U. S. Centers for Disease Controls and Prevention. (2016). *Violence against children in Nigeria: Findings from a national survey.* Nigeria.

Nandy, S., & Pomati, M. (2015). Applying the consensual method of estimating poverty in a low-income African setting. *Social Indicators Research, 124*(3), 693–726. https://doi.org/10.1007/s11205-014-0819-z.

Ozoemenam, K., Ekanem, A., & Delamonica, E. (forthcoming) Perception of child poverty in southern Nigeria: Children's voices. *Journal of Poverty,* 1–21. https://doi.org/10.1080/10875549.2021.1910103.

Pomati, M., & Nandy, S. (2020). Measuring multidimensional poverty according to national definitions – Operationalising target 1.2.2 of the sustainable development goals in Benin, Gabon, Guinea, Liberia, and Mali. In: Nebie et al. (eds.) *Child poverty and social protection in Western and Central Africa.* CROP and Ibidem-Verlag

Pomati, M., Nandy, S., Angemi, D., Gordon, D., Depio, S., Ahaibwe, G., Kasirye, I., Muwonge, J., Ssennono, V., Baryahirwa, S., Twesigye, B., Eroglu-Hawksworth, S., Fahmy, E., Oloya, A., & Fifita, V. (2020) Multidimensional child poverty and the SDGs: From measurement to action. In D. Lawson, D. Angemi, & I. Kasirye (eds.) *What works for Africa's poorest children: From measurement to action.* Practical Action Publishing.

Powell, M. A., Taylor, N., Fitzgerald, R., Graham, A., & Anderson, D. (2013). *Ethical research involving children.* Innocenti PublicationsUNICEF Office of Research – Innocenti.

Qvortrup, J. (1993). Societal position of childhood: The international project childhood as a social phenomenon. *Childhood, 1*(2), 119–124.

Truscott, J., Graham, A., & Powell, M. A. (2019). Ethical considerations in participatory research with young children. In A. Eckhoff (ed.) *Participatory research with young children. Educating the young child* (Advances in theory and research, implications for practice), 17. Springer, Cham. https://doi.org/10.1007/978-3-030-19365-2_2.

4 Children's Citizenship in Twenty-first Century Societies: Key Notes from the South

Damián Molgaray

4.1 Introduction

As an introduction to this chapter, it is important to acknowledge the impossibility to thoroughly determine in what way, and through what means, the citizens exercise a significant political agency in increasingly complex societies. In general lines, the construction of citizenship—as well as the criteria applied for their inclusion—has lacked uniformity, since the theories of citizenship have undergone transformations in the context of an arena where different semantics are in dispute, thus resulting in a variety of temporary definitions.

The incipient literature on childhood citizenship, with a clear predominance of north-western countries, could be classified within two large fields of approach to citizenship: some authors place more emphasis on the differentiated peculiarities of the legal status of the child in connection to political communities, while others explore various social initiatives or practices marked by children's participation and protagonism.

Nevertheless, the social and political phenomena that occur in many Southern countries of the planet offer a reality which calls for a particular analysis, resulting in special meanings of the term citizenship. Weak institutionalization processes and unconsolidated democracies offer temporary visions of citizenship, from incomplete democratization thresholds, visualizing experiences of agencies that operate with a marginal performance, or from conflictive environments. In addition, the widespread sense of global risk, economic crises, or the disintermediation offered by social networks, Southern countries grapple with complex realities such as urban violence, unsatisfied basic social rights, and generalized loss of faith

D. Molgaray (✉)
CICS-Universidad de Palermo, Buenos Aires, Argentina

G. Tonon (ed.), *Re-defining Children's Participation in the Countries of the South*, Kindheit – Bildung – Erziehung. Philosophische Perspektiven,
https://doi.org/10.1007/978-3-662-64167-5_4

in politicians, all of which has an impact on the deployment of citizenship of adults and, especially, on children.

On the basis of a technical approach on bibliographic analysis, and resorting to examples derived from the author's research work, this chapter aims at making a contribution of innovative ideas which will allow a deeper insight into possibilities and limitations of child citizenship from the perspective of the South. Thus, we shall begin by introducing some brief notes on the concept of citizenship, followed by an approach on the complexity of the precarious citizenship–childhood relationship, and eventually delve into the limitations and new expressions detected from the Southern countries. This will be rounded off by conclusions on the subject, to encourage reflection.

4.2 Concept of Citizenship: Brief Notes on Its Evolution

According to Wolin (2012), the concepts that form part of the technical political vocabulary have been designed to adjust to the theoretical frameworks. These political terms are the universal glossaries (from the Western World), which are subtly intermingled with philosophical ideas and notions about the use of space and the conception of time (Wolin, 2012).

It is in this context that the political concept of citizenship emerges. Although, at this stage, it would be impossible to display a detailed evolution of the concept of citizenship; it is deemed suitable to go over the nature of this term, tracing some of its most interesting essential traits, with the object of applying them, later on, to the complex conception of child citizenship.

The roots of the concept of citizenship are so deep, that they date back to Ancient Greece. On a first approach, it may be asserted that citizenship was usually related to the actual exercise of political rights. In the times when the Ancient Greek Poleis were the nucleus of human existence, life in the city entailed an intensely political association in which "visual power" predominated, thus displaying close interpersonal bonds (Wolin, 2012, p. 103).

With the passing of time together with the growing complexity of the societies of the Western World, the aforementioned conception of citizenship—characterized by its horizontal and territorial bonds—gradually lost its strength. The expansion of Roman culture, by mutating the dimensions of the communities, represented the shift from an intimate political relationship to "abstract politics," in other words, political distancing (Wolin, 2012, p. 103). The practicality and penetration of Roman Law all over Europe became the source of inspiration of what would later be defined as the modern liberal tradition which sustains republican forms of government (Milne, 2013). The novelty introduced by the Roman formula had the effect of amplifying the citizens' rights through the principle of equality under the law (Bellamy, 2008).

The irruption of national States (by the end of the XVII century), led to the nation-state construction, as a fictional contraption, a useful tool to homogenize the political life of sovereign territories. The figurative conceptualization of nation, halfway between the values that radiated from the Greek nation-state and the great Roman Empire (Bellamy, 2008), constituted—according to Anderson (1993)—a type of community of imaginary characteristics, which attempted to overcome the social differences inherent of cultural heterogeneity.

Bourgeois revolutions, together with the expansion of liberal ideologies, returned to a philosophy centered in people's individual rights, so far subjugated by the State powers (negative liberty), thus recovering the ideal of self-government (Greek) through the strength of elections in representative democratic regimes (Przeworski, 2010), thus setting the foundations of the modern interaction between the political class that constitutes the State, and through which public policies are set in motion.

Nevertheless—regarding the rights of a nation to elect its own representatives—it was not until the XX century that citizenship acquired a universal significance, i.e., that this right became extensive to all its members. In this sense, according to Bellamy (2008), the development of a more inclusive citizenship is in keeping with the expansion of a welfare state founded on civic equality. In fact, during the 1950s, the Marshall Plan (1950) raised awareness of the impossibility to enjoy full citizenship—i.e., civic and political participation—if certain social conditions, related to material resources to ensure a decent lifestyle, were not previously guaranteed.

According to the scheme contributed by Lizcano Fernández (2012), it may be stated that the modern trend has outlined two clear conceptions of citizenship, at least in the Western World: an embracing citizenship which legitimates the condition of the inhabitants as members of a sovereign territory, offering a number of minimum rights to all people; and another category, regarded as inclusive–exclusive, which grants and extends rights to a certain portion of the population, in order to encourage their involvement in public administration. On the other hand, Borja (in Lizcano Fernández, 2012) states that nationality is a condition inherent of citizenship (not the other way around), and that the rights derived from that condition must be placed at two different levels: on the one hand, social and civil rights, common and inherent to all human beings and, on the other, political rights reserved for politically active persons depending on the following: being of age, having a full nationality, and no legal restrictions.

There are two basic elements in the nature of citizenship which seem to have been kept over the centuries. One of these elements is status (generally known as normative legal), which determines the right to extended formal national membership (involving the enjoyment of certain rights, services, and guarantees); the second element is the subjects' possibility and permanent disposition for participation in the public sphere (not necessarily in the formal political/governmental field), which activates the subjective awareness of being (and feeling) an active part of the community, by taking part in the preparation or management of public affairs (Espinosa 2009).

4.3 Childhood and Citizenship: A Complex Issue

Like many of the academic debates on citizenship held all through history, the principle of children's citizenship arose from heated arguments born of social movements and political readjustments, eventually deriving in the inclusion of the figure of the child on the national and international political agenda. This began in the second half of the XX century, when a series of declarations and international agreements were drawn to promote and protect childhood. The International Convention on the Rights of the Child, born of an initiative of UNICEF supported by the United Nations in 1989, was the first binding international agreement that unified, in a single text, the right of a child to enjoy full childhood in a specific social group.

Furthermore, almost simultaneously with the signing of the Convention on the Rights of the Child, a new branch of Sociology, known as Sociology of Childhood, began to be developed with the aim of achieving recognition for boys and girls as subjects of rights and as social actors with competence in the social structure, with genuine potentiality to interact with other generations in society. By highlighting the articles of the Convention which promoted children's right to participation, this line of thought contributed to the generation of a series of sociopolitical debates (still unconcluded) on the concept of citizenship and the way it relates to childhood as a social group (Ramiro & Alemán Bracho, 2016).

Going back to the above-mentioned scheme proposed by Lizcano Fernández (2012), children's rights to citizenship could be regarded as passive citizenship, which owns a distinctive feature, i.e., the recognition of the civil and social rights inherent to their condition as human beings.

Nevertheless, the traditional status of full citizenship (which includes political rights) relegates young people to a situation of dependence with regard to their families—and State institutions—on the assumption that this age group is incapable of taking on the same responsibilities as the rest of the citizens (adults). This denial of a recognition of their political prerogatives (the right to vote in particular) is, according to Milne (2013). the reason why children are entitled to an incomplete citizenship, which explains why modern democracies—with some exceptions—have a tendency to exclude children from processes involving community decision-making, even when those decisions might affect their own lives.

Mieles Barrera and Tonon (2015) point out that, in regarding childhood as a mere process in the development of a person to become an adult, (i.e., as a transition to adulthood), one tends to overlook the definitive traits of the child (boy or girl), together with their related potentials—as part of a social, political, cultural, and economic context—which enable them to build their own biographies. Thus, the term "minor" reaffirms the typical negative representation of childhood which situates these subjects as forming part of a stage of life characterized by incapacity to reason or undertake responsibilities. Being a minor is a condition which, according to Gaitán Muñoz (2006), entails children's subordination to a dominant group, resulting in discrimination which affects their agency and rights of participation, merely on the grounds of their young age.

Thus, regarding legal obligations, there are two coexisting theories on childhood citizenship, with different nuances. While one of these theoretical positions claims equality rights for children to develop to their full capacity, the other—of a more moderate liberal core—(more in keeping with the principles of the Convention on the Rights of the Child) proposes favoring the roles of childhood citizenship, by promoting their participation, while at the same time, providing them with the guarantees of protection they require under the primary responsibility of their families (Ramiro & Alemán Bracho, 2016).

Perhaps this tension between participation and protection or, in other words, between greater freedom vs greater care and assistance, is the dynamics which has characterized the complex process of children's citizenship, both in theoretical and practical terms. How can these two "typical" (or we had better say "key") elements of citizenship fit into the spaces of childhood?. How can children's status as members of a community that offers recognition and protection coexist with the systematic limitation of their real options of participation generated by the dependency derived from increasing protection? One of the causes of this tension is perhaps the (extremely dangerous) tendency to treat children as though they were adults (Lister, 2007a).

The current of thought which proposes the construction of a substantive citizenship for children has come to release these tensions by acknowledging the fact that—quoting Lister (2007a)—some of the fundamental axes of the concept of citizenship are, in all cases, less compatible with childhood. Thus, the aforementioned line of thought recognizes citizenship as a dynamic reality, generated from practice. (Romero & Alemán Bracho 2016). Within that focus on childhood citizenship, two other positions coexist: namely differentiated citizenship and lived citizenship.

Taking as reference the social and identarian movements of the 1960s, differentiated citizenship proposes public recognition of individual differences and particular necessities. This outlook grants a (special) differentiated recognition of certain non-hegemonic identities. Thus, certain marginal groups are allowed to preserve their identities and cultural habits in their public lives (Young, 2000). According to Moosa-Mitha (2005, p. 386), this new conception of citizenship extends the right to be "differently equal" while interacting with other diverse social groups.

While differentiated citizenship appeals to deconstructive discourse, thus revealing a more combative attitude which aims at vindicating the potential of children's insights, which remain invisibilized in the public agenda, lived citizenship—on the other hand—shreds that discourse in order to analyze the significance that adults tend to attribute to children's agency in citizenship. Thus, lived citizenship focuses attention on children's life experience and their possibilities for participation—formally or informally—thus institutionalizing their views in decisions affecting their lives (Romero & Alemán Bracho 2016).

The substantive trend mainly encourages a more inclusive perception of citizenship, through which it may be possible to enhance those socio-political practices oriented to social recognition and a shared identification (Lister, 2007b). Regarding the stage of childhood, then, the practice of citizenship is a source of interest, for it does not presuppose a predefined path, thus integrating children and therefore recognizing the legitimacy of their status as actors in the public sphere (Lawy & Biesta, 2006).

Several experiences in the South may serve as an example of the dynamics of substantive citizenship, particularly in Latin America, where the empowerment of feminist groups has served as a model in the vindication of egalitarianism (Lister, 2007a). In this respect, it is worth mentioning care workers' responsibilities which are often undertaken by the very young—particularly by girls—as a clear example of the equal conditions and engagement imposed by reality, both for adults and children alike (Lister, 2007a) (especially in the great number of contexts in which socio-economic deprivation predominates). This situation exposes the actual possibilities that exist in these contexts, thus calling for a reformulation of the uniform criteria which shapes the traditional norms for adult, white male citizenship (Lister, 2007a). In this respect, Liebel (2017) highlights the way in which post-colonial proposals invite a reinvention of the concept of citizenship, by taking into account the citizenship practices displayed by children in their daily life spaces in the global South; practices which—more often than not—are not in keeping with the typical conception of citizenship consolidated in the traditions of the Western World. The spaces for children's organization and cooperation, which seek visibility among the political actors for the recognition of their rights of participation—as in the case of the associations of working children in Latin America—set an example of concrete initiatives originated in the South, with the aim of achieving autonomy over their own decisions, thus quenching the thirst for participation that emerges from the bases of society (Liebel, 2006).

In this context, therefore, the two main trends related to childhood citizenship under consideration (legal and substantive) may be understood as reflection paths, which sometimes converge and, on other occasions, run in parallel.

It is particularly interesting to observe how the substantive trend has gained approval among the countries of the global South. It is possible that the positions which are averse to the dominant idea of a liberal Western citizenship may be the clues to understand the growth of this theoretical innovation in the South. Likewise, the limitations undergone by a great part of the population, with relation to the possibility of enjoying and exercising basic rights (including those contemplated by law), may be other reasons for this overflow of participation toward the banks of a "legitimate" political arena.

By placing less emphasis on legal conventions—and more on socio-political practices—the substantive outlook on citizenship allowed the display of a multilevel (and multidisciplinary) analysis which expanded the scope of citizenship beyond the axes determined by the national States, thus allowing studies on different scales (Lister, 2007b). These studies have shed light on valuable experiences of "non conventional" citizenship, especially in the world of childhood.

The following section will seek to point out some peculiarities of the political reality of Latin American States: starting from the premise that the mixture of local idiosyncrasies together with the complex democratization process that the societies of this region are going through (living under a republican model, shaped by the core principle of liberalism), there is a consequent limitation in the display of full citizenship, affecting the options of (re)thinking people's condition as citizens in general, and of childhood in particular. Moreover, some social phenomena that took place in the late XX century and early XXI century—which coincide with the recognition of children as subjects of rights—have established dichotomous realities in this region where, for instance, a stronger presence of the State and a progressive display of democratic discourse coexists with cases of deep social disintegration and a growing social vulnerability.

4.4 Limits and New Experiences of Citizenship: Some Key Trends from the South

As we have mentioned above, it is not surprising that many experiences from the South should reflect some traits of substantive citizenship, on account of the great number of experiences of activist demonstrations detected among the Latin American population—not in keeping with the traditional concept of citizenship. According to Meltzer and Rojas (2014), the limits of citizenship in Latin America have been configured according to racial, spatial, or class hierarchies. Though civil and political freedoms have been formally acknowledged in the Constitutions of the Latin American republics, in actual fact the citizens of this region have been claiming for equality of opportunity and substantive social guarantees, for decades (Meltzer & Rojas, 2014). Weak democratic institutionalization, together with recurrent economic crises—deriving in long term unemployment rates in the region—has brought about increasing apathy and disbelief among the citizens, together with an ever growing intolerance to the unlawful processes of impoverishment they have become immersed in (Nieto, 2017). In fact, Hoevel (2015) identified distrust as an intersubjective factor which pervades the disagreement with, or the systematic non-fulfillment of the regional norms, which evidently hinder institutional stability.

The legitimacy achieved by the democratic discourse spread through the Latin American States—particularly as the aftermath of the authoritarian experiences of the 1970s and 1980s—has not succeeded in putting an end to spoil systems in national politics—to the point that these practices (at different levels) seem to have reached all the social groups (Nieto, 2017). In this context, we should add the ever present violent reminiscences of the darkest years of military dictatorships, still lurking in the region.

In the early 1990s, Lechner (1994) had already noticed the distrust generated by the general impression that the political system cannot control social processes. And when, in turn, politics fails to implement contingency management, individuals are invaded by a feeling of uncertainty, thus generating a gap between personal expectations and public matters. Faced with isolation, the citizens end up perceiving politics as a personal activity, which weakens the bonds they need in order to nurture their political belonging, and consequently generating greater indifference toward public affairs.

Moreover, according to Garland (2005), the crisis of the end of the XX century confronted societies, worldwide, with permanent disorder resulting in the breakdown of collective identities and the preeminence of market power abuse over the (presumably) consolidated rights of the citizens. As a complement, the emergence of globalization contributed to dissipating the figure of the political community in the whole planet (Bellamy, 2008). In this regard, the difficulties experienced by Latin America to sustain, at a minimum, the framework of protection that social citizenship requires—in the style proposed by Marshall (1950)—are a proof of this, not to mention the dismantling of the basic social achievements obtained by some of the countries in this Continent during the post-World War II period (Freijeiro Varela, 2008).

What makes this situation so alarming is that it excels the concern for State institutions; for it is a warning against the latent danger that lurks behind the future of political activity in contemporary societies. If—as we anticipated—citizenship is founded on the basic rights of a nation and, if public space is defined as the environment which offers multiple opportunities of social contact, consequently, the deterioration of the "communicating vessels" which allow us the possibility of "being with others," together with public sphere alienation, will invariably lead, on the one hand, to a breakdown of a collective sense of belonging, and on the other, to a decrease in the citizens' involvement and participation in initiatives which tend to cater for the necessities and claims of a community.

The multiple elements which have been briefly taken into consideration clearly show the complex and paradoxical situation undergone be the idea (or promise) of a full exercise of citizenship all over the world, and particularly in Latin America, where the processes of institutional instability and idiosyncrasies characterized by informal employment complicate the social and political situation of these days—which seems to have come to stay. It is clear that citizenship is neither a product of rhetoric or decree. The limits of the substantive implementation of rights over adult citizens, naturally, casts doubts over the possible access to citizenship of the child. Is it possible to conceive childhood citizenship in this region, when this condition is even alien to the adult population?.

According to (Ramiro & Alemán Bracho, 2016), resorting to the aforementioned legal trend on citizenship does not make much sense when it comes to analyzing daily childhood experiences in this region—even though this trend (even to this day) supports the discourse which aims at enhancing positive rights for children. The driving force that frequently places citizenship as "what ought to be" (the finish line) often overlooks the effects of the portion of that citizenship which "is not," i.e., (an alien in the present circumstances), thus the deferred legal action that this trend denounces with regard to childhood, would also—paradoxically—apply to the situation of many adults who have, intermittently, become imperfect citizenship subjects. Is that not obvious?

There is data which supports the above-mentioned views. A report issued by the international organization Save the Children (2018) has observed that, though most Latin American States are making an attempt to abide by the international norms to guarantee children's condition as subjects of rights, the legal frameworks still sustain the old conceptions of the doctrine of Irregular Situation and, to make matters worse, the same political class further encourages legal reform processes which—if applied—would profoundly affect the existing childhood rights. Moreover, the same report raised the alarm regarding the way in which most of the plans and programs that constitute public policies in the region continue to reproduce models that cut down on shortage assistance—essentially unfavorable to children's active participation—thus leaving these experiences to the philanthropic commitment of some private Civil Society Organizations.

On the other hand, the focus of substantive citizenship allows the discovery of logics of social and political citizenship that differ from the ones that have, so far, been in force in Latin America—logics which, in the complexity of the above-mentioned context, do not seem to be contributing to the achievement of greater social inclusion. In spite of the fact that new minorities are still eager to occupy public spaces, it is evident that this eagerness goes hand in hand with an alarming tendency toward the privatization of private services, political delegitimation, and a decline of public space. This phenomenon of growing polarization becomes more obvious in light of childhood life experiences.

A brief reference to some of the field research results obtained by the author of this chapter would be enough to demonstrate how boys and girls of different socio-economic origins in the Buenos Aires Metropolitan Area (Argentina) currently mention episodes or situations which cause them to feel unsafe in their city for they regard the street dangerous due to the number of intoxicated reckless drivers, heated arguments in the streets, not to mention countless criminal acts. Similar situations have been reported by Vera and García (2005) from Colombia, where childhood citizenship is threatened by fear, thus generating indifference and skepticism regarding political participation. This reality may be found all over the region, with different nuances, according to the peculiarities of each context. Orozco et al. (2020), for instance, analyzed the social representations of boys and girls living in settlements where drug trafficking is rampant in a city situated in the Pacific coast of Mexico; while Niño (2019), from Colombia, made an attempt to understand the processes leading to the construction of political subjectivity in boys, girls, and youngsters living in contexts of armed violence in the city of Cúcuta.

Though there is not so much research work on the subject, the preliminary approaches show that the children's fear exposes the difficulty they find in socializing in a public context that has turned menacing, therefore "pushing" them, and their families, to seek hospitality and interpersonal exchange in the intimacy of private places. The hazards that children find in public spaces—mostly related to the streets—are counteracted by small communities related to club life, school, or the family circle, which are described by boys and girls as small secure places or containment zones. It must be added that, in this context, "community" refers to the social link based on intersubjective ties such as: affection, sense of belonging in a community or a neighborhood, territorial proximity, and friendship (Tonon, 2017). In the words of Tonon et al. (2017), the aforementioned phenomenon is more explicitly found in the typical lifestyle of big cities.

The gradual loss of civic virtue among citizens has negative effects on urban life. The failure of citizen participation in urban life leads to exclusion, isolation, and seclusion from public space—especially affecting that most need secure quality public space; children in particular (Borja, 2003). Going back to Lechner (1994), we may wonder about the limits of the sense of belonging in a political community when the citizens appear to be scattered in small concrete and particular circuits. Hoevel (2015) again refers to small, unstable networks lacking in reciprocity to be found in Latin America, limited to a certain (controlled) radius of trust, which nurtures a social capital rich in relationships, but always circumscribed to close affinity and family ties. The nuclearization of the families offers an alternative to the subjects' community dismemberment. This explains why the home—according to Palacio Valencia (2010)—has turned into a space to escape from the adversities of the public sphere.

The state of affairs we have, so far, described is somewhat bleak. It puts forth a complex situation which, though it may be dismissed—for being regarded as an overview of the situation—the diverse social realities of many children in each country also discloses the difficulties undergone by many minorities in the region, including the case of children who "take to the streets," on the one hand, to obtain public recognition and gain more political rights, and on the other, to further enjoy social and economic guarantees from the State, as a means of becoming part of the social network.

Nevertheless, it is important to highlight that the subjects' tendency to isolation into the private sphere do not necessarily imply mere political activism from marginal spaces, or the least total "resignation" of their personal aspirations (though this may, clearly, happen). When consulted about their fears, in qualitative research studies, the children from Buenos Aires express their subjectivity when they acknowledge their daily life experiences in society. The fact that they are able to admit their fears, born of the menacing worldly reality of their own lives (and the lives of others)—opens up a wonderful opportunity to consider them as a potential source that may allow these deficiencies to be turned into overcoming collective action (Lechner 2002/2015).

In this regard, we may make reference to a category studied by Plummer (2001), called "intimate citizenship" which, though it was originally coined as a means of calling attention to the incidence of sexuality in determining the vindication of new rights in the sphere of citizenship; it also served the purpose of pointing out the beginning of a novel phenomenon through which the concerns which were traditionally restricted to the adults' public sphere (especially regarding their body), began to expand into an ever growing individualistic public sphere. In the case of childhood, intimate citizenship gives way to a multilevel analysis through which it is possible to recover children's spaces where—in the midst of the complexities of the societies they live in—they are able to carry out more or less autonomous activities which allow them to interrelate and feel identified with their peers, only in environments that may offer them comfort and a sense of safety. In this regard, we ought not to overlook the fact that the spaces which adults normally regard as "adequate for" children are not always in keeping with the places the children regard as "theirs"—in other words, the environments that boys and girls describe and define as their own (Rasmussen, 2004).

According to (2013), the duties and responsibilities assumed by the citizens in modern societies have become a source of support and stability for the social groups, which explains why citizenship might also be analyzed as individual freedom, co-responsible for the future of a community, as well as for community vitality, which allows greater sharing of public spaces (Lechner, 2000). Unfortunately, the progressive deterioration of public space in Latin America gives an inkling of the generalized structural crisis derived from modern society; those very same structures, which do not seem to have completely adapted to this region, no longer generate a sense of co-responsibility for a common future and widespread social bonds while, on the other hand, there seems to be a growth of fragmented private associations. Therefore, in the case of children, their use of digital social networks is becoming increasingly obvious and these connections occur at school or during extra-curricular and sports activities, a sort of "reprimarization" or privatization of third places.

Though it is true that these peculiarities, typical of children's intimate lives, do not have a direct repercussion on the public sphere—as in the case of the social phenomena mentioned by Plummer (2001)—they might be incipient citizenship experiences, almost regarded as romantic, as compared to the crudeness of the current State of affairs, thus intertwining alternatives to their personal and collective future, from the safety of a certain environmental containment. In other words, though citizenship generally refers to a specific form of participation through which individuals become an integral part of the political community through the free exercise of their rights and responsibilities in order to take part in decision-making concerning public affairs, in their own interest (Espinoza, 2009), truth to tell, when it comes to children, the conditions of the socio-political environment and idiosyncrasies, prevent a greater display of participation in public space while the forms of community integration fail to find intergenerational "connecting vessels."

The aim of this proposal, far from attempting to annul, let alone set limits, to the existing vindications of full citizenship—both for children and adults—acknowledges the need for an effective coexistence between normativity and concrete citizen participation experiences. Nevertheless, it proposes a more realistic outlook on the present situation in the South, thus recovering the children's sincere and unprejudiced discourse, through which they make their opinions plain, take sides, and argue about their authorities, about public policies, and about the problems in the contexts they live in.

Quoting the thoughts of María Elena Walsh (1956), a famous Argentine writer, devoted to literature for children: "in a world which spoils the privileged and exempts them from responsibilities, we are melancholic since our early childhood, preferably in a garden, and that is the lie that drains our vitality. (...) Maybe we overlook the fact that all children are serious (...) they are always beyond the nonsensical prison cell in which we attempt to lock them up in order to conceal the truth from them." Enhancing the strength of the children's discourse, even in private environments, might recreate an appropriate context in which, as in ancient societies, active listening and intimate conversations may become the pillars of true citizenship for—and from—childhood.

4.5 Conclusion

The aim of this research work is to contribute some innovative clues in order to probe deep into the limits and possibilities of childhood citizenship in the South. After revising the concept of citizenship, and dwelling on the complexity of citizenship and childhood, this chapter has highlighted how—by placing less emphasis on legal conventions, and greater emphasis on socio-political practices—the substantive trend of thought allows a multilevel (and multidiscipline) analysis, in order to expand the field of citizenship beyond the axis determined by the national State, thus opening a door to research studies at different scales.

The political realities of Latin American States, especially Argentina, characterized by complex and devious democratic processes, together with certain socio-economic phenomena that took place in the late XX century and early XXI century (exactly coinciding with the recognition of the child as a subject of rights) have resulted in the hindering of full citizenship, thus affecting the possibility to reconsider people's status of citizens in general, and of children in particular.

This chapter has further attempted to identify children's spaces where—amid the complexities of the societies they live in—they succeed in carrying out more or less autonomous activities, and where they are able to interrelate and identify themselves with their peers, yet mostly in safe and comfortable environments. Paying attention to these dynamics, which take place in children's "private," or personal environments, might be one of the keys to collecting particular socialization experiences—typical of the Southern reality—through which it may be possible to detect children's sense of belonging and solidarity, setting aside foreign categories which, in most cases, are far removed from the (truly intricate) realities of this part of the world.

References

Anderson, B. (1993). *Comunidades imaginadas*. Fondo de Cultura Económica.

Bauman, Z. (2007). *Miedo líquido: la sociedad contemporánea y sus temores*. Paidós.

Beck, U. (2008). *La sociedad del riesgo mundial*. Paidós.

Bellamy, R. (2008). *Citizenship: A Very Short Introduction*. Oxford University Press.

Borja, J. (2003). *La ciudad conquistada*. Alianza Editorial.

Espinoza, M. (2009). La participación ciudadana como una relación socio-estatal acotada por la concepción de democracia y ciudadanía. *Andamios, 5*(10), 71–109.

Freijeiro Varela, M. (2008). ¿Hacia dónde va la ciudadanía social? (de Marshall a Sen). *Andamios. Revista de Investigación Social, 5*(9), 157–181. http://dx.doi.org/https://doi.org/10.29092/uacm.v5i9.188
Gaitán Muñoz, L. (2006). El bienestar social de la infancia y los derechos de los niños. *Política y Sociedad, 43*(1), 63–80.
Garland, D. (2005). *La cultura del control: crimen y orden social en la sociedad contemporánea.* Gedisa editorial.
Hoevel, C. (2015). Raíces del problema institucional argentino: Una reflexión. *Revista Cultura Económica, Year XXXIII, 90*, 44–59.
Lawy, R., & Biesta, G. (2006). Citizenship-As-Practice: The educational implications of an inclusive and relational understanding of citizenship. *British Journal of Educational Studies, 54*(1), 34–50. https://doi.org/10.1111/j.1467-8527.2006.00335.x
Lechner, N. (1994). Los nuevos perfiles de la política. Un Bosquejo. *Nueva Sociedad, 130*, 32–43.
Lechner, N. (1999/2015). Los desafíos de la gobernabilidad en una sociedad global. In I. Semo, F. Valdés Ugalde & P. Gutiérrez (Eds.), *Obras IV: política y subjetividad, 1995–2003/ Norbert Lechner* (pp. 101–115). Fondo de Cultura Económica-FLACSO.
Lechner, N. (2000). Nuevas ciudadanías. *Revista de Estudios Sociales*, (5). https://doi.org/10.7440/res5.2000.03
Lechner, N. (2002). Nuestros miedos. In M. I. Villa Martínez (Ed.), *El miedo: reflexiones sobre su dinámica social y cultural* (pp. 135–155). Corporación Región.
Lechner, N. (2002/2015). Las sombras del mañana. La dimensión subjetiva de la política. In I. Semo, F. Valdés Ugalde y P. Gutiérrez (Eds.), *Obras IV: política y subjetividad, 1995–2003/ Norbert Lechner* (pp. 187–284). Fondo de Cultura Económica.
Liebel, M. (2006). Los movimientos de los niños y niñas trabajadores. Un enfoque desde la Sociología. *Política y Sociedad, 43*(1), 105–123.
Liebel M. (2017) Children Without Childhood? Against the Postcolonial Capture of Childhoods in the Global South. In A. Invernizzi, M. Liebel, B. Milne, & R. Budde (Eds.), *Children Out of Place' and Human Rights. Children's Well-Being: Indicators and Research (79–97).* Vol. 15. Springer. https://doi.org/10.1007/978-3-319-33251-2_6
Lister, R. (2007a). Why citizenship: Where, when and how children? *Theoretical Inquires in Law, 8*(2), 693–718.
Lister, R. (2007b). Inclusive citizenship: Realizing the potential. *Citizenship Studies, 11*(1), 49–61.
Lizcano Fernández, F. L. (2012). Conceptos de ciudadano, ciudadanía y civismo. *Polis. Revista Latinoamericana, 11*(32), 269–304.
Marshall, T. (1950). *Citizenship and social class.* Cambridge University Press.
Meltzer, J., & Rojas, C. (2014). Transformations in imaginings and practices of citizenship in Latin America. In E. F. Isin & P. Nyres (Eds.), *Routledge Handbook of Global Citizenship Studies* (pp. 253–264). Routledge. Taylor & Francis Group.
Mieles Barrea, M. D., & Tonon, G. (2015). *Calidad de vida y niñez: Perspectivas desde la investigación cualitativa.* Universidad de Magdalena.
Milne, B. (2013). *The History and Theory of Children's Citizenship in Contemporary Societies.* Springer.
Moosa-Mitha, M. (2005). A Difference-Centred Alternative to Theorizing of Children's Rights. *Citizenship Studies, 9*(4), 369–388. https://doi.org/10.1080/13621020500211354
Nieto, N. (2017). La corrupción en América Latina (1976–2016). *Episteme, 9*(1–2), 75–85.
Niño, N. C. (2019). La calle y el barrio como entornos violentos y espacios de subjetividad política de niños, niñas y jóvenes en la ciudad fronteriza de Cúcuta [Monografía]. *Sociedad e Infancia, 3*, 65–82. https://doi.org/10.5209/soci.63502
Orozco, R., Sánchez Arellano, E., Torres Osuna, C., & Camacho Castro, G. (2020). Representaciones sociales de niñas y niños acerca de su barrio en un contexto de narcotráfico [Monografía]. *Sociedad e Infancias, 4*, 55–67. https://doi.org/10.5209/soci.68021
Palacio Valencia, M. C. (2010). Los tiempos familiares en la sociedad contemporánea. La trayectoria de una configuración. *Revista Latinoamericana De Estudios De Familia, 2*, 9–30.

Plummer, K. (2001). The square of intimate citizenship: Some preliminary proposals. *Citizenship Studies, 5*(3), 237–253.
Przeworski, A. (2010). *Qué esperar de la democracia: límites y posibilidades del autogobierno.* Siglo XXI editores.
Rasmussen, K. (2004). Places for children-children's places. *Childhood, 11*(2), 155–173.
Ramiro, J., & Alemán Bracho, C. (2016). ¿El surgimiento de un nuevo sujeto de ciudadanía? Aportaciones teóricas al debate contemporáneo sobre los derechos de los niños. *Papers. Revista De Sociología, 101*(2), 169–193. https://doi.org/10.5565/rev/papers.2218
Tonon, G. (2017). Rethinking community quality of life in Latin American Countries. In G. Tonon (Ed.), *Quality of Life in Communities of Latin Countries* (pp. 3–14). Springer. https://doi.org/10.1007/978-3-319-53183-0_1
Tonon, G. H., Benatuil, D., & y Laurito, M. J. (2017). Las dimensiones del bienestar de niños y niñas que viven en Buenos Aires, Argentina. *Sociedad e Infancias, 1*, 165–183. https://doi.org/10.5209/SOCI.55330
Vera, M. J., & García, L. H. (2005). Imaginarios de ciudadanía en niños y niñas: ¿súbditos o empoderados? *Investigación & Desarrollo, 13*(2), 296–317.
Wolin, S. (2012). *Política y perspectiva: continuidad e innovación en el pensamiento político occidental.* Fondo de Cultura Económico.
Young, I. M. (2000). *La justicia y la política de la diferencia.* Cátedra.

Other sources consulted

United Nations (UN), General Assembly. Resolution 44/25. Children's rights convention. Approved November 20th 1989.
Save the Children (October, 2018). *Mapeo sobre legislación y políticas en países en América Latina y el Caribe referidas a la participación de niños, niñas y adolescentes en la toma de decisiones.* Managua. https://resourcecentre.savethechildren.net/node/14317/pdf/mapeo_legislacion_y_politicas_lac_participacion_nna_en_toma_de_decisione.pdf.
Walsh, M. E. (1956). *La seriedad de los niños.* La Gaceta de Tucumán.

Children's Rights and Participation in School in South Africa

5

Irma Eloff and Daniël J. Eloff

5.1 Introduction

The aim of this chapter is to explore conceptualisations of child[1] participation in the South African education sphere. It sets out to provide a legal perspective on the frameworks that provide for children's participation and identifies limitations and challenges to children's participation in the school context. It also provides an education perspective on children's participation by highlighting the emphasis on access to education in an emerging democracy (which, in some ways, is to the detriment of participation in education). We argue that access to education should concurrently imply participation in education, since in its absence, learning outcomes at both the individual and systemic levels may be affected. The chapter concludes by connecting the notion of participation in education with the Global Goals for Sustainable Development.

[1] The chapter uses both 'child' and 'student', depending on the context of the discussion. The term 'child' is used predominantly for the legal perspective, and 'student' is used for the educational perspective.

I. Eloff (✉)
Department of Educational Psychology, University of Pretoria, Pretoria, South Africa
e-mail: irma.eloff@up.ac.za

D. J. Eloff
Department of Law, Akademia, Pretoria, South Africa
e-mail: daniel@akademia.ac.za

G. Tonon (ed.), *Re-defining Children's Participation in the Countries of the South*, Kindheit – Bildung – Erziehung. Philosophische Perspektiven,
https://doi.org/10.1007/978-3-662-64167-5_5

5.2 A Legal Perspective

As South Africa approaches nearly three decades of democracy and 25 years of a new constitutional dispensation, the country still faces daunting challenges to ensure that the freedoms enshrined in the Constitution, Act 108 of 1996 (RSA, 1996) are realised. Although children (as defined in the Constitution) do not have the right to vote or hold public office, they do enjoy most other civil and political rights guaranteed to all citizens. Children have the right to freedom of expression, the right to join and form a political party, the right to peacefully assemble, to demonstrate, to picket and to present petitions, and the right to participate in the law-making process, just as all adult South Africans.

South Africa's 1996 Constitution guarantees specific protections and freedoms for children. For the first time in history, South Africans are ensured that '*a child's best interests are of paramount importance in every matter concerning the child*' (RSA, 1996, Section 28(2)), as the Constitution has positively resulted in advocacy for children's rights and the development of legal protections for children in particular. What ensued has in broad terms promoted children's civic participation and independent decision-making and resulted in mandatory consultation processes that require child participation (Moses, 2008). The phrase 'every matter concerning the child' requires the best interest of the child to be considered while bearing in mind the child's ability to meaningfully participate in matters concerning them (e.g. schools and educational institutions).

These national constitutional protections for children were preceded by the United Nations Convention on the Rights of the Child (Office of the High Commissioner of Human Rights, 1989) which sets out the civil, political, economic, social, health and cultural rights of children. For purposes of this chapter, we focus particularly on articles 12 and 13 of the Convention, which guarantee children's participation rights by ensuring they are afforded the opportunity to express their views freely and that their views are assured due weight in accordance with their age and maturity. Moreover, the 1999 African Charter on the Rights and Welfare of the Child provides similar freedoms of expression, association and thought. These international mechanisms, in conjunction with the developing body of South African law, increasingly ensure that the voices of children are heard in a country with a history of injustice and disregard for individual agency.

5.3 Defining children's participation in South Africa

Hart (1992) describes children's participation as 'the fact of being involved in the decision-making that concerns oneself and that concerns the life of the community in which one lives'. This is not only a recognition of children's inherent interest in matters that concern them, but also an acknowledgement of their ability to influence matters that concern them. Consequently, children's participation rights involve having a voice as well as a choice in processes and decisions that affect them (Parkinson & Cashmore, 2008). The growing acknowledgement that children not only ought to be heard but that their voice can substantially contribute to decision-making that affects them has inspired the continued development of South African law to address current hindrances that exclude effective and enabling participation by children. Despite encouraging steps that have been taken, many challenges unfortunately remain within the country and its judicial system.

One of the key characteristics of the children's rights guaranteed in the South African Constitution is its focus on protection (Moses, 2008). This protection-orientated nature likely stems from the dependency of children and the limited status granted to children in society. It created a general framework that viewed children as objects of protection rather than as individuals with rights and accompanying agency. Moreover, the Constitution itself is silent on direct protections that ensure children participation and focuses largely on negative rights, i.e. rights that prohibit particular actions. The term 'right' in this context simply means to be entitled to a particular thing and to be protected against any deprivation or denial that will constitute an injustice (Myers, 2017). Negative rights, therefore, ensure that children are not subjected to the actions of other individuals or authority by prohibiting the use of force or coercion when consent is not given. The lack of acknowledgement of children's agency is a shortcoming that has to be addressed. Even in terms of the strictest and narrowest philosophical worldviews, writers agree that children's rights, including the right to participate in the conducting of their own affairs, are of utmost importance (Sorens, 2001).

The South African Constitution does not directly mandate or require children's participation on any governmental level, but as mentioned above, it overarchingly provides that the best interest of the child is paramount. Moreover, it dictates that children enjoy all the freedoms guaranteed in the South African Bill of Rights. The Constitution obliges that all spheres and levels of government in the country must allow for public participation in the legislative and policymaking processes. The 'public' includes children, and therefore, children have guaranteed (and arguably accentuated) rights to public participation (Viviers & Lombard, 2013).

5.4 Existing Framework for Children's Participation

5.4.1 The Constitution of the Republic of South Africa, Act 108 of 1996

Although the South African Constitution does not directly and fundamentally protect children's participation rights, it does provide for a rights-based regime that ensures protection of the individual autonomy and agency of children. Section 28 of the Constitution contains a Bill of Rights for children within the main Bill of Rights. The section starts off with the phrase 'every child' and is followed by a list of nine particular rights that all children enjoy, in addition to the rest of the rights enshrined in the Bill of Rights. Importantly, this section's protection is afforded not only to children as individuals but also as a marginalised and minority group (Reyneke, 2013). Our courts have interpreted Section 28 in broad and accommodating terms in order to include virtually every single matter that affects a child.

In light of the South African Constitution being the supreme law in the country, many children's rights, including the right to participation, are ancillary rights rather than explicit rights guaranteed in the text of the Constitution. The Constitution therefore empowers national legislation, and it compels the incorporation of international law, including the United Nations Convention on the Rights of the Child and the African Charter on the Rights and Welfare of the Child, to ensure that a child's right to participation is adequately, beneficially and progressively realised. Flowing from the Constitution, the Children's Act and South African Schools Act ensure a broad range of rights, including participation rights for children within the educational context.

5.4.2 Children's Act 38 of 2005

Flowing from Section 28 of the South African Constitution, the Children's Act was enacted in 2005 with one of its core functions aiming to provide children the opportunity of substantial participation. This includes participation not only in their own affairs but also substantial participation in the affairs of our constitutional democracy (Davel & Skelton, 2007). It concurs with the view that children should be allowed and empowered to participate in the broadest possible terms (Lücker-Babel, 1995). The Children's Act consequently provides for the right of children to express their views freely; it determines their role in evolving capacities, outlines the areas where the views of children have to be considered, determines how these views should be heard and provides children both access to South African courts and the means to enforce their rights.

Although the South African Constitution does not explicitly define children's participation, the Children's Act, which is a national piece of legislation, defines and uses the term 'the right to participate' in Section 10. Particularly, this section of the Act provides that '*every child that is of such age, maturity and stage of development as to be able to participate in any matter concerning that child has the right to participate in an appropriate way and views expressed by the child must be given due consideratio*n'.

Pursuant to the children's rights enshrined in the Constitution, the Children's Act is applicable to all children, regardless of their status as citizens of South Africa. The protection granted in the Children's Act is therefore extended to children of immigrants and foreign nationals, regardless of whether they legally reside in the Republic of South African. The universal protection ensured by the Children's Act is undoubtedly a positive development in that it ensures that the most vulnerable children, namely those of immigrant parents, are also protected.

The participation rights of children listed in the Children's Act are, however, subject to certain provisions regarding the child's age, maturity and stage of development. In fact, Section 6(3) of the Act provides that '*the child's family must be given the opportunity to express their views*'. Thus, the Act aims to ensure that decisions that affect children are taken with due consideration of the views and best interest of the child, while ensuring consummate weight being given to their views. Another important aspect regarding a child's right to participate is that the Children's Act does not only require child participation within the vertical relationship between the state and a child, but the Act actually mandates child participation within their own families and communities. Section 31(1)(a) of the Children's Act reads '*before a person holding parental responsibilities and rights in respect of a child takes any decision ... involving the child, that person must give due consideration to any views and wishes expressed by the child, bearing in mind the child's age, maturity and stage of development*'. The Children's Act expressly requires that the views of children be considered with a vertical application as well, i.e. that the views of children should matter not just between individuals but also when it comes to interactions between the state and the child. The Children's Act therefore provides for broader and encompassing decisional autonomy beyond that endorsed by the United Nations Convention on the Rights of the Child and the African Charter on the Rights and Welfare of the Child (Moyo, 2015).

5.4.3 South African Schools Act 84 of 1996, and Provincial Schools Acts

With the transition to democracy in South Africa, the newly elected democratic parliament of South Africa enacted the South African Schools Act (SASA) in an effort to transform the South African school system (De Waal et al., 2001). Initially, the focus was placed on ensuring access to education and removing institutional and societal barriers that hampered equitable access to the South African educational system (Woolman & Fleisch, 2009). Despite the fact that SASA has since addressed many of the structural and other challenges, South Africa still faces major challenges to ensure that children's voice be heard within their own school context.

Currently, participation within the local school context largely involves community participation by way of elected school governing bodies (SGBs) that represent the schooling community. SGBs enjoy 'a position of trust', and therefore, these bodies have considerable autonomy while working with the school as well as with provincial and national education departments (Woolman & Fleisch, 2009). Their involvement in the affairs of schools ensures representative and direct participation (Woolman & Fleisch, 2009). SGBs are constituted predominantly by the parents of learners who are currently enrolled in the school. These duly elected parents have various derived powers in terms of SASA, which empowers them to act in the interest of the schooling community and the learners at large.

In terms of South African law, school governing bodies are considered duly elected organs of state. In terms of Section 41 of the Constitution, all organs of state, from the executive right through to school governing bodies, have a duty to adhere to the principle of cooperative governance (Serfontein & De Waal, 2013). The principle of cooperative governance ensures that decision making at school level cannot take place without proper consultation of the school community, who is represented through the school governing body. Combined with the fact that school governing bodies are given considerable autonomy, the majority of most influential court cases regarding educational matters in South Africa nowadays involve school governing bodies litigating on behalf of the schooling community and children and quite successfully too.

Despite the prominence given to school governing bodies—admittedly a positive development—this has not necessarily resulted in children's voices being heard meaningfully. Neither SASA nor any other piece of legislation directly mandates that the voices of children and their inputs be duly considered (Reyneke, 2016). Although SASA as a post-apartheid piece of legislation achieved a great deal with regard to other problems that plagued the South African schooling system, there remains room for improvement in realising the rights of children to meaningfully participate in matters that concern them—such as their schools. Despite the obligations imposed by both the South African Constitution and the Children's Act, meaningful child participation within their own educational context is currently still limited. Some degree of effort has been made to ensure that children are provided fair and transparent opportunity to have their voices heard, particularly in school disciplinary matters that concern them (Reyneke, 2016). However, if proper regard is to be given to the rights enshrined in the South African Constitution, then such rights cannot merely remain within the realm of disciplinary matters. Child participation consequently has to progress beyond mere involvement in their own disciplinary cases to also include meaningful engagement that extends beyond formal procedural aspects of education. It should also include participation in school governance and cooperative governance that give appropriate weight and consideration to the views of children.

SASA does not obligate and advocate the same individual autonomy of children as is upheld in the South African Constitution. It is therefore argued that SASA, in conjunction with the various provincial schools acts, should be read with sufficient regard given to the rights of children to participate. Importantly, these participation rights should be viewed in two particular regards: firstly, in terms of individual participation, and secondly, in terms of collective participation by groups of students.

The South African Constitution provides a rights-based and systematic legal framework that should be interpreted as ensuring and enhancing particular freedoms and participation (Van Staden, 2020). The Constitution, through its protection of participation rights as well as enunciated children's rights, should be used and read in such a manner as to ensure individual autonomy and meaningful participation by children within their school context. South African courts have been largely silent on the theme of children participation within the school context. Moreover, precedent regarding children participation in the broader sense is limited to a few cases regarding child participation in school disciplinary matters. There is room for innovative and ground-breaking law making and litigation to extend child participation in school contexts, considering that the Constitutional Court held the following view in the case of *S v M* regarding the constitutionally protected best interest of children:

> The word 'paramount' is emphatic. Coupled with the far reaching phrase 'in every matter concerning the child', and taken literally, it would cover virtually all laws and all forms of public action, since very few measures would not have a direct or indirect impact on children, and thereby concern them.

The Constitutional Court therefore unambiguously holds that the best interest of a child and therefore the child's ability to meaningfully participate in their school context are paramount in all matters concerning the child. Efforts therefore have to be made to ensure more and better participation by children in the school context, while applying the appropriate level of weight and consideration, depending on the age of the child (Reyneke, 2013). Despite the unambiguity in the Constitution, numerous cases exist where child participation in schools was largely ignored, whether deliberately or not. In these cases, it would undoubtedly have been advantageous to ensure that the views of children be heard, and potentially, the views of children could have assisted the courts in coming to equitable and just conclusions.

In the case of *Organisasie vir Godsdienste-Onderrig en Demokrasie v Laerskool Randhart and Others,* the High Court in Johannesburg was confronted with the question of religion in schools. In this case, the applicants took six schools with religious practices and the national Department of Education to court, seeking that the court should declare unconstitutional a range of defined propositions. These included schools associating themselves with any particular religion and permitting religious observances as part of the school programme. Despite the fact that the very central question of the litigation concerned the tension between religious rights of religious and non-religious children, the views of the children involved were never sought.

Similarly, in the case of *Head of Department: Mpumalanga Department of Education and Another v Hoërskool Ermelo and Another,* the Constitutional Court heard a case that concerned the right to receive education in the official language of one's choice in a public educational institution. As in the case above, the central legal question at hand and the consequences of the court's finding directly affected the learners of the school as well as learners in various other schools across the country, due to the precedent that the case created. Child participation never formed part of the court process in this case either (It must be pointed out that, regardless of the courts' conclusions, the fact that direct child participation was neglected cannot be justified).

Although great strides have been made towards meaningful child participation, the value of the South African legal framework that provides for participation rights can only be truly measured through tangible change. Our legal framework empowers and allows for meaningful child participation within the school context, which is a first step in the right direction. If the protections and ambitions of our rights-based constitutional dispensation are to be realised, the individual autonomy of children and their ability to meaningfully engage in matters that affect them have to be adequately acknowledged. Moreover, perceptions about children's ability to meaningful contribute and engage have to be transformed. Although our legal framework, in conjunction with international law, undoubtedly assists in achieving these lofty and noble goals, the true measure of success is squarely vested in the willingness of parents, schools, teachers and children themselves to give effect to these rights.

5.5 Educational Perspective

Access to education has been a key driver for educational policy and governance during the transition to a democratic dispensation in South Africa (Fiske & Ladd, 2004; Soudien, 2011). Globally, access to education is viewed as a powerful lever for alleviating poverty, reducing inequality, promoting health, increasing gender equity and improving quality of life (Giannini, 2020; Nielsen, 2006; UNESCO, 2020b). In the first two decades of democracy in South Africa (1994–2014), significant investment has been made to increase access to education (Bloch, 2008; Spaull et al., 2016; Van der Berg et al., 2016). Starting with the Foundation Phase, through to higher education, more students have accessed educational opportunities and more students (in actual numbers) have completed their schooling in comparison to prior years. However, while broad access to education has increased, questions are increasingly asked about the quality of educational opportunities across the socio-economic spectrum, and concerns are raised about high dropout rates in vulnerable groups (Weybright et al., 2017).

Even though significant gains have been made, it must be conceded that access to education does not necessarily equate to participation in education. From a legal perspective, participation in education is conceptualised in terms of student agency and the presentation of student voice in matters of governance, policy making and legislation. The educational perspective on participation in education, in turn, engages the process of teaching and learning itself and positions the student as an active agent in learning. Within this perspective, it is acknowledged that a child might have access to education, but not necessarily be participating in education processes.

In this regard, it should be noted that the continuum of functional and dysfunctional schools is wide-ranging in the South African school sector and therefore closely related to student participation in education. Reports on teacher absenteeism and limited 'time on task' by teachers are often presented (Bipath et al.,

2019). At the same time, the socio-economic factors that impact student participation, student engagement and school attendance remain pervasive. Daily participation in school is hampered by long distances to be walked to school, lack of learning materials, the burden of HIV/AIDS, language barriers, orphanhood and various other systemic factors.

In addition to existing restraints, access to and participation in education have been impacted severely for all South African children during the COVID-19 pandemic. Various levels of national lockdown and intermittent school closures since the start of the pandemic have meant that millions of students lost access to education at school sites (Van der Berg & Spaull, 2020). Access to learning opportunities from alternative sites and home environments presented with substantial challenges for most students. While highly functional schools have been able to move their teaching and learning to online environments, low-resource schools have experienced severe challenges in making learning accessible for their students. In many ways, the pandemic has exacerbated existing inequalities and impacted participation in education severely for the most vulnerable students.

5.6 Sustainability, Participation and Knowledge Democracy

Indications are that within the first year of the global COVID-19 pandemic, significant impediments have been reported to the attainment of the Global Goals for Sustainable Development (United Nations, 2021). More than half of the world's student population (800 million+students) experienced significant disruptions to their schooling, ranging from 'full school closures in 31 countries to reduced or part-time academic schedules in another 48 countries' (UNESCO, 2021) during 2020. High levels of variance also occurred in terms of the duration of school closures, depending on world regions. On average, schools around the world were closed for periods of between 14 and 22 weeks (UNESCO, 2021).

The immediate adverse consequences of school closures during the COVID-19 pandemic were evident globally since the advent of national lockdowns. Besides the direct effects of school closures on teaching and learning, negative effects in respect of child nutrition, elevated stress levels for teachers, pressure on childcare options, high economic costs and an unintended strain on healthcare systems have been documented (UNESCO, 2020c). Concerns about widening inequality have been expressed around the world in various sectors of society (Armitage & Nellums, 2020; Dorn et al., 2020). In South Africa, the concerns about exacerbated inequality as a result of school closures and national lockdown levels have been specifically pertinent.

However, in many ways, the COVID-19 pandemic has provided opportunities for educational renewal at the systemic level. Previously, large-scale education interventions have been challenging for many reasons but perhaps most prominently because of the risks involved in 'experimenting' with an entire generation of students. The pandemic has forced deep reflection on education systems and participation in education, and it has accelerated the use of technology, online learning and digital resources for teaching and learning in all phases. The challenge now is the creation of pathways for all students to access education and to participate optimally in quality education.

In considering the importance of optimal participation rates in education, immediate concerns such as learning losses, student dropout rates and indirect adverse effects on health outcomes in children presented during the pandemic. There is, however, also a longer-term consideration when participation rates in education decline, namely the setback in terms of the development of knowledge democracy (Hall & Tandon, 2020) around the world.

In the long term, plurality of knowledge serves society and supports systemic solutions during times of crisis. As such, Jourdan et al. (2020, p. 172) argue for the harnessing of an inherently plural 'combination of different kinds of knowledge within an 'educational pathways' framework to make education relevant and equip learners with the skills to tackle the societal challenges of the future'. When participation rates in education decline or fluctuate, learning losses and depressed growth in knowledge democracy can be expected.

Nevertheless, Hall and Tandon (2020, p. 23) argue that

> ...[k]nowledge democracy principles can be readily incorporated into the futures of education. Essentially, this practice translates to learning to respect learning in the classroom as well in everyday life. There are practical ways that knowledge democracy can be promoted within existing education systems. In primary levels of education, it will entail a further push to incorporate interactive learning in the real world (i.e. learning from life). At the secondary level, education syllabi can be framed around clusters of societal challenges. In post-secondary education, both teaching and research can be causally linked to developing socially responsible professionals and experts. The use of community-based participatory research methodologies by students and teachers can promote respect for local knowledge and co-construction of research.

Increasing participation in education beyond the mere notion of 'access' can expand the knowledge democracy and signify the plurality of knowledge that will be needed to face the complex challenges of the future. Access to education should therefore be coupled with and followed by participation in education. Investments in expanding access to education should also provide for the creation of robust pathways for participation in education for all children.

Since investment in education extends well beyond direct educational outcomes, it has been alarming to note the remark in the Global Education Monitoring report, which indicates that '[e]ducation budgets declined after the onset of the Covid-19 pandemic in 65 percent of low- and lower-middle-income countries compared to only 33 percent of high- and upper-middle-income countries' (Education Finance Watch, 2021, p. 8). This in indicative of an intensified detrimental effect on the targets of several of UNESCO's sustainable development goals—not only the SDG regarding quality education. The anticipated outcomes in respect of no poverty (SDG1), zero hunger (SDG2), reduced inequalities (SDG10), and peace, justice and strong institutions (SDG16) will also be affected by reductions in education expenditure and consequently a decrease in participation rates in education.

5.7 Conclusion and the Way Forward

What is the way forward? The global COVID-19 pandemic has illuminated several shortcomings in respect of child participation in education in the South African context. It has also inadvertently demonstrated the unique strengths aimed at protecting the rights of children that emerged from a Global South country during a time of social and political disruption. These strengths include the robust utility of the law, heightened public awareness on quality education, the advancement of a collective responsibility for education, and a redefinition of the notion of a school. There has been a rethinking of educational pathways for all students and the importance of lifelong learning opportunities has been re-emphasised.

References

Armitage, R., & Nellums, L. B. (2020). Considering inequalities in the school closure response to Covid-19. *The Lancet Global Health, 8*(5), 644.

Bipath, K., Venketsamy, R., & Naidoo, L. (2019). Managing teacher absenteeism: Lessons from independent primary schools in Gauteng, South Africa. *South African Journal of Education, 39*(Supplement 2), 9, 1–9.

Bloch, G. (2008). *Investment Choices for South African Education.* Wits University Press.

Chirwa, D. M. (2002). The merits and demerits of the African Charter on the rights and welfare of the child. *The International Journal of Children's Rights, 10*(2), 157–177.

Davel, C. J., & Skelton, A. M. (2007). *Commentary on the children's act.* Juta.

De Waal, E., Theron, T., & Robinson, R. (2001). An education law analysis of the learner's best interests. *Perspectives in Education, 19*(4), 151–161.

Dorn, A. V., Cooney, R. E., & Sabin, M. L. (2020). Covid-19 exacerbating inequalities in the US. *Lancet (london, England), 395*(10232), 1243–1244.

Education Finance Watch. (2021). *Global education monitoring report*, ED/GEM/MRT/2021/EFW/1, 1–20.

Fiske, E. B., & Ladd, H. F. (2004). *Elusive Equity: Education Reform in Post-Apartheid South Africa.* Brookings Institution Press.

Giannini, S. (2020). *Say no to discrimination in education, join the 1960 convention as it turns 60.* UNESCO.

Hall, B., & Tandon, R. (2020). Knowledge democracy: Opening our doors to all knowledge systems. In: UNESCO, *Humanistic futures of learning*. United Nations Educational, Scientific and Cultural Organization.

Hart, R. A. (1992). *Children's participation: From Tokenism to citizenship* (No. inness 92/6).

Jourdan, D., Faucher, C., Cury, P., Lamarre, M-C., Mebtoul, M., Matelot, D., Diagne, F., & Damus, O. (2020). Plurality of knowledge to meet the challenges of tomorrow. In: UNESCO (ed.), *Humanistic futures of learning.* United Nations Educational, Scientific and Cultural Organization.

Lücker-Babel, M. F. (1995). The right of the child to express views and to be heard: An attempt to interpret Article 12 of the UN Convention on the Rights of the Child. *The International Journal of Children's Rights, 3*(3–4), 391–404.

Moses, S. (2008). Children and participation in South Africa: An overview. *The International Journal of Children's Rights, 16*(3), 327–342.

Moyo, A. (2015). Child participation under South African law: Beyond the convention on the rights of the child? *South African Journal on Human Rights, 31*(1), 173–184.

Myers, P. C. (2017). *From natural rights to human rights and beyond.* The Heritage Foundation.

Nielsen, H. D. (2006). *From schooling access to learning outcomes: An unfinished agenda – An evaluation of world bank support to primary education*. World Bank Publications.
Office of the High Commissioner of Human Rights. (1989). *Convention on the rights of the child.* UN General Assembly Resolution 44/25. United Nations.
Parkinson, P., & Cashmore, J. (2008). *The voice of a child in family law disputes*. Oxford University Press on Demand.
Porsdam, H. (2020). Science as a cultural right. In: UNESCO (ed.), *Humanistic futures of learning*. United Nations Educational, Scientific and Cultural Organization.
Republic of South Africa (RSA). (1996). *The Constitution of the Republic of South Africa 1996.* Government Printers.
Reyneke, M. (2013). Children's right to participate: Implications for school discipline. *De Jure Law Journal, 46*(1), 206–236.
Reyneke, M. (2016). Realising the child's best interests: Lessons from the child justice act to improve the South African schools act. *Potchefstroom Electronic Law Journal/Potchefstroomse Elektroniese Regsblad, 19*(1).
Serfontein, E. M., & De Waal, E. (2013). The effectiveness of legal remedies in education: A school governing body perspective. *De Jure Law Journal, 46*(1), 45–62.
Sorens, J. (2001). Libertarian theory and children's rights: The fiduciary model, rationality, interests and the challenge of abortion. *Philosophical Notes*. Libertarian Alliance.
Soudien, C. (2011). Quality's 'others'?: The politics of bordering and re-bordering our educational standards. *International Review of Education/internationale Zeitschrift Für Erziehungswissenschaft/revue Internationale De L'education, 57*(3–4), 261–275.
Spaull, N., Van der Berg, S., Wills, G., Gustafsson, M., & Kotzé, J. (2016). *Laying Firm Foundations*. Stellenbosch University.
UNESCO. (2020a). *Humanistic futures of learning*. United Nations Educational, Scientific and Cultural Organization.
UNESCO. (2020b). *60 Years of the UNESCO convention against discrimination in education – What happened since the adoption?* United Nations Educational, Scientific and Cultural Organization.
UNESCO. (2020c). *COVID-19 education response: Preparing the reopening of schools* (resource paper). United Nations Educational, Scientific and Cultural Organization.
UNESCO. (2021). *UNESCO figures show two-thirds of an academic year lost on average worldwide due to Covid-19 School closures*. United Nations Educational, Scientific and Cultural Organization.
United Nations. (2021). *About the sustainable development goals*. (Accessed 2 March 2021). https://www.un.org/sustainabledevelopment/sustainable-development-goals/.
Van der Berg, S., Spaull, N., Wills, G., Gustafsson, M., & Kotzé, J. (2016). *Identifying Binding Constraints in Education*. Stellenbosch University.
Van der Berg, S., & Spaull, N. (2020). *Counting the Cost: COVID-19 School closures in South Africa & its impacts on children*. Stellenbosch University.
Van Staden, M. (2020). Constitutional rights and their limitations: A critical appraisal of the COVID-19 lockdown in South Africa. *African Human Rights Law Journal, 20*, 484–511.
Viviers, A., & Lombard, A. (2013). The ethics of children's participation: Fundamental to children's rights realization in Africa. *International Social Work, 56*(1), 7–21.
Weybright, E. H., Caldwell, L. L., Xie, H. J., Wegner, L., & Smith, E. A. (2017). Predicting secondary school dropout among South African adolescents: A survival analysis approach. *South African Journal of Education, 37*(2), 1–11.
Woolman, S., & Fleisch, B. (2009). *The Constitution in the classroom: Law and education in South Africa, 1994–2008*. PULP.

Purpose for Power (P4P). Participation as a Way of Being and Becoming in Haiti: A Practical Approach to Genuine Empowerment, and Well-being Among Young People

6

Cornelia C. Walther

6.1 Introduction

Today is the steppingstone for tomorrow. We know more and have more are more connected and dispose of greater access to explore what we do not know yet. At the same time, COVID-19 has made it evident that not everyone benefits from the treasures of these times. Genuine participation remains a faraway dream in (too) many places as the evitable inequitable gap between rich and poor is widening. The cracks of deprivation run across the globe. In all countries, the pandemic has pulled the veil of a systemic social paradox whereby everyone is at risk to get sick physiologically speaking, yet where not only the outcomes of such sickness depend on a person's socioeconomic standing due to the ability to afford care; but also, the risk of getting exposed in the first place (Walther, 2020c). COVID shines a spotlight on the dramatic imbalance that characterizes our societies.

Individual well-being is the cause and consequence of collective well-being. A society where individuals are lifted to fulfill their potential represents a space of shared opportunity that benefits everyone in it. Such a space is not Utopia, but it requires the empowerment of everyone to participate in the local and national sphere.

Yet to participate in life must not depend on affordability—participation reached beyond material considerations. (Sect. 6.1).

The aim of *Purpose for Power* (P4P) is not to make participative solidarity 'fashionable' but normal. Rather than requesting individuals to do something or

C. C. Walther (✉)
Muenster University, POZE_ezop, Tübingen, Germany

G. Tonon (ed.), *Re-defining Children's Participation in the Countries of the South*, Kindheit – Bildung – Erziehung. Philosophische Perspektiven,
https://doi.org/10.1007/978-3-662-64167-5_6

another, the goal is to make them *want* to do it, by nurturing their desire of joining a social cause. The methodology guides young people, through their caregivers, toward gradual autonomy. It offers a different take on self-identity based on connections. P4P optimizes the interplay of inner resources and social circumstances; while showing links between personal well-being and action that is taken for the well-being of others.

What follows is anchored in the POZE paradigm.

POZE has various meanings. In particular, it reflects the paradigm's 1) Parameters: Purpose (the innate quest for meaning which expresses the human soul), Om (the universally recognized word of emotional harmony), Zoom (a focus on the essential), Expression (the translation of our inner reality in the World); 2) Outcomes: Perspective (a holistic view on life), Optimization (through influence on the dimensions that shape existence), Zenith (the pursuit of our best self), Exposure (the exploration of unknown solutions). The noun 'Poze' translates as 'inner peace' in Haitian Creole where the approach that is presented in this chapter was prototyped in 2017, triggering an expanding network of likeminded thinkers and doers (People On Zenith Exploration).

Every individual has the resources for a meaningful and fulfilling life. Access to this innate potential begins, when people identify the underlying aspiration of their existence. 'Empowerment' in the POZE perspective—means to find, feel, understand and pursue this aspiration. Based on the understanding that human existence is a composite of four dimensions—aspirations, emotions, thoughts and sensations (Sect. 6.2), the *Purpose for Power (P4P)* approach enables individuals to participate fully wherever they are, independently of their age, gender, socioeconomic context and overall environment. Such genuine participation is addressed as being central to subjective well-being and collective prosperity (Sect. 6.3). It helps individuals help themselves and others. P4P guides participants to understand the dimensions that impact their experiences and behavior, while offering them tools to influence these dimensions consciously. Central to this process are the answers to four questions—Why (Purpose), Who (Personality), Where to (Situation) and What (Action). In Haiti, P4P was used to train teachers and social workers working with children and adolescents in order to also address education and thus empower the next generation to participate from an early age.

The orientation toward proactive participation, and the quality of the overall educational experience is critical. It stresses the importance of the social and interactive processes of learning (Dewey, 1938). Yet the mainstream education system is mostly based on traditional pedagogy, following a 'banking model of education which treats the student as an empty vessel to be filled with knowledge' rather than treating the learner as a co-creator of knowledge (Freire, 1970). Trained in such a unilateral manner, students tend to grow up to be citizens without skills or appetite to participate in their community; they lack the desire to critically question the status quo. Without an aspirational anchor, they gradually enter the desires and dictates of Society. Rather than shaping reality through active participation, they consume it. Rather than questioning the meaning of their existence (Why), while shaping their unique personality (Who), they get drawn down into the societal hamster-wheel of doing and desiring; concentrating on the pursuit of priorities that others have chosen for them. This context is not favorable to the rise and growth of creative minds; it does not nurture individuals who are ready to envision, build and participate proactively in Society. Education must establish the link between aspirations and action (What), between possibility and participatory pursuit (Where).

The main hypothesis of P4P and the main message of this chapter is that the status quo, where inequity and indifference are condoned or overcompensated, can, and must, be challenged. Using the POZE paradigm, P4P offers a sustainable approach that can be applied everywhere, by anyone; using local resources, and expertise to address the four W's. The underlying logic is that aspiration for meaning is the central driver of human decision making.

Identifying and defining the unique contribution that individuals aspire to make is the starting point for everything that follows; it equips them with the power to participate fully, in their life and that of other ones. Because once they identify WHY they aspire to life and begin to pursue their purpose, individuals gradually access and share their innate potential. In that process, they nurture their own resilience and that of their community. An outline of the application of P4P in Haiti serves to illustrate the steps and results (Sect. 6.3).

The chapter concludes with a summary of elements for further discussion; including a call to look beyond categories to people, beyond sectors to the optimization of resources for lasting outcomes. Aim is to contribute to the growing understanding amid educators and aid practitioners that siloed work is inefficient and often harmful when the overall ambition is to empower individuals to participate. While this perspective has grown in theory, it is yet to be translated into systematic practical changes, to impact the planning and implementation of pedagogic curricula (Sect. 6.4).

6.2 Context

Everything is connected. Quality of life ensues when the aspirations, emotions, thoughts and physical experience of individuals are in synch (Walther, 2020b). This inner harmony, or lack thereof, finds its reflection in the relationship of individuals with their environment. Thus, investing in individuals with a holistic angle, addressing the material and immaterial components that impact their well-being, benefits the community they live in. Creating a future where people across the social spectrum have a fair chance to participate in life and living, hereby fulfilling their inherent potential begins with systematic investments in the mindset of young people, and those who care for them; this must include tools to nurture a participative attitude. The factors that shape their existence today determine the quality of life that Society will enjoy tomorrow. In the Quality-of-Life System Theory Structure, quality education represents a component for quality of life (Hagerty et al., 2001, p. 80). It is also included in the Convention on the Rights of the Child (Article 12):

> 1. States Parties shall assure to the child who is capable of forming his or her own views the right to express those views freely in all matters affecting the child, the views of the child being given due weight in accordance with the age and maturity of the child. 2. For this purpose the child shall in particular be provided the opportunity to be heard in any judicial and administrative proceedings affecting the child, either directly, or through a representative or an appropriate body, in a manner consistent with the procedural rules of national law.

The right of all children to be heard and taken seriously constitutes one of the fundamental values of the Convention. The Committee on the Rights of the Child (the Committee) has identified article 12 as one of the four general principles of the Convention, the others being the right to non-discrimination, the right to life and development, and the primary consideration of the child's best interests, which highlights the fact that this article establishes not only a right in itself, but should also be considered in the interpretation and implementation of all other rights (UN Committee on the Rights of the Child (CRC), General comment No. 12 (2009): The right of the child to be heard, 20 July 2009, CRC/C/GC/12).

Since the adoption of the Convention in 1989, considerable progress has been achieved at the local, national, regional and global levels in the development of legislation, policies and methodologies to promote the implementation of article 12. A widespread practice has emerged in recent years, which has been broadly conceptualized as 'participation', although this term itself does not appear in the text of article 12. This term has evolved and is now widely used to describe ongoing processes, which include information-sharing and dialogue between children and adults based on mutual respect, and in which children can learn how their views and those of adults are taken into account and shape the outcome of such processes.

Taken together, the rights contained in the International Convention of the rights of the child (CRC) are more than the sum of their parts. A person's *potential* encompasses aspirational, emotional, mental and physical aspects, which must be conjointly addressed to unfold. The four pillars of the CRC—Survival, Education, Protection, Participation—represent a connected quartet. Programs in each of these areas can serve as entry-points to further a happy healthy childhood, if they are conceived with the understanding of their mutual complementarity. A panoply of development and humanitarian programs have been conducted without such synergy, leading to duplication, waste of resources and limited impact where efficiency and progress would have been essential to build and nurture a sustainable state of individual well-being and collective welfare. Both contribute to and derive from resilience (Sanders et al., 2015). Participation is often addressed as an afterthought, rather than a central pillar that influences the sustainability of the others.

6.3 Material Versus Immaterial Factors of Development

Whereas some perceive our mind and consciousness as byproducts of material processes (such as the biochemistry of the human brain and nervous system), (Novak, 1979), and by extension see society as a derivate of material means;

others consider consciousness as a first-order reality to which matter is subject and material interactions are secondary (Guyer & Horstmann, 2015). POZE aligns these contrasting views within the perspective that mind and matter, individual and collective not only influence each other mutually, but depend onto each other within a continuum of complementary change to overcome the unnecessary suffering that derives from inequity. Both components must be addressed consciously and in the understanding of the interplay so that genuine participation can happen. This perspective goes further than the capability approach (Sen, 1979), which offers alternatives to welfare economics, using microeconomic techniques to evaluate well-being (welfare) at the aggregate (economy-wide) level—because it does not only stress the central place of individual empowerment, but offers why and how such empowerment is the cause and consequence of genuine participation.

Over the years, an economic growth has left millions of individuals to face discrimination, and deprivations due to their race, ethnicity, skin color, identity and gender. Despite impressive gains in expanding social services during the last few decades, people continue to die, be illiterate and oppressed due to avoidable causes. In an age of abundance, they face deprivation. Looked at from a perspective of connected dimensions, the status quo is not caused by an overall lack of means, but an imbalance between needs and means which has localized consequences. However, if inequity is the problem to be solved than the root cause to overcome is not the lack of material means but the mindsets that are behind their distribution. Sustainable human development depends on the participation of everyone in the generation and enjoyment of life and living. Change outside requires change inside. Offering everyone a fair opportunity to identify and fulfill their inherent potential requires an understanding of the interplay between purpose and power, between empowerment and participation in society.

Genuine participation is a central factor for quality of life. The latter looks at material and immaterial factors, in the pursuit of physical, mental and social well-being (Michalos, 2015; Fayers & Machine, 2007). It includes everything from physical health, family, education, employment, wealth, safety, security to freedom, religious beliefs and the environment. Hereby, it bridges the divide between moral and material considerations.

A 360-degree understanding of the environment that individuals evolve in may appear radical when contrasted to the simplistic growth models. But society evolves with the mindsets that evolve in it. 'Thinking that bifurcates moral on the one hand and material on the other is inhibiting. But such thinking is not natural and inevitable, it is mutable and contingent—learned and apt to be unlearned' (Sen, 2009).

6.4 Participative Education Models as Catalysts of Change

A growing number of academics and aid practitioners, of citizens and politicians around the world see the weakness of the current unilateral system.

But for change to occur, individuals must not only acknowledge that the situation is wrong, they must care enough to get involved and see opportunities to do so. Change requires (com)passion and the use of existing and new resources. Such a mindset can be nurtured from childhood; education that is geared toward participation is an investment in a new generation. COVID-19 exposed a social conundrum that has persisted for decades. The world has enough resources to cover everyone's needs, but as already stated by Gandhi, not enough to cover everyone's greed. The prevailing reality has negative consequences on the individual, from death over disease to disillusionment and depression, and on society, from loss of social cohesion over violence to stagnating prosperity—because a context of exclusion prevails where only some can and want participate consciously in the dynamics that shape their present and future. These circumstances suggest that a paradigm shift is needed. The 'bystander effect' refers to a behavior pattern, whereby individuals are less likely to help someone in need when other people are present; the greater the number of bystanders, the less likely it is that one of them will help (Hudson & Bruckman, 2004). COVID-19 was a stark reminder that individuals around the world must step out of their bystander attitude and participate in their world. Change is overdue, and so is the return to meaning.

Across cultures, continents and centuries, humans have been driven by the quest for meaning. Purpose more than power, pleasure or possessions drives mental health, personal well-being, collective resilience (Sirgy, 2002, Kauffman, 2016); and, more than anything else, it fuels genuine participation. Caring for a cause cultivates individual progress and nurtures social advancement. It is the main characteristic that distinguishes individuals from each other, and from animals. Aspiration allows a person to not only bounce back from hardship but to transcend hardship and inspire others to follow their example.

Purpose gives power to participate. It is a central component of mental health, underpinning our subjective perception of well-being. When purpose is missing mental distress ensues. Mental distress has physiological consequences, such as pain or disease, whereas biological factors such as nutritional deficiency or illness have an impact on a person's mood and performance. This circle extends beyond the individual, to the environment they live in. Whether passively or proactively we inflict our inner state of mind on others—in the case of teachers and caregivers, this affects the children they work for. Conversely, living and working in a challenging environment causes stress and anxiety, and in more severe cases loss of purpose and depression. The dynamic operates from the inside out—from aspirations to experiences, and from the outside in—from experiences to aspirations. Both affect human behavior, or our ability to participate in the forces at work that influence us, while being influenced by us in return.

Resilience—Empowerment—Participation

These three words have been over-used until they lost meaning; joining the catalogue of other important yet emptied wordy words such as 'vulnerability' [vulnerable to what? We are all vulnerable to some-thing]; 'beneficiary' [the passive connotation of the word is at best incorrect, and more often insulting to the person who is referred to as such] and 'participation' [child participation is not done justice when children are placed on a podium to be photographed, nor if they are trained to repeat political statements and platitudes]. In the present chapter, we refer to *Resilience* as the ability to overcome challenges and thrive not despite but because of them. *Empowerment* is addressed one the one hand with an individual connotation, as a path for persons to identify and pursue the purpose of their existence, the cause that gives them passion and through it the power to thrive; on the other hand, it will be looked as in the collective dimension where a critical mass of individuals has found and begun to pursue meaning. It is a question that matters universally, from high- to low-income locations. Herein *Participation* refers to the act of joining with others in doing something. Empowered individuals participate in their life and make a difference in that of others; this renders them resilient to external and internal stressors.

Peoples across the World struggle with very different material challenges, yet individuals face the same craving for personal meaning and for social connection; operating within an ever-evolving continuum of complementarity. The quest for 'happiness' unites people and peoples around the world (Wierzbicka, 2004; Waterman, 1993). It relates to mental or emotional states, including positive or pleasant emotions ranging from contentment to intense joy (Schwartz, 2006); but also relates to the life satisfaction, subjective well-being, eudaimonia and well-being. In the present chapter, it is referred to as a state of inner peace.

The overall hypotheses which underpin the approach that is presented in this chapter looks at the individual and the collective level:

Individual—If individuals learn to identify and pursue their personal aspirations; using and nurturing the resources which they have already, while proactively seeking additional ones, then they are equipped to recover from hardship (resilience) and take on a proactive stance in their life and that of others (empowerment).

Collective—When a critical mass of individuals with that mindset lives within a given society, then social commitment becomes the norm (Bicchieri, 2008). Indifference and competition are replaced by compassion and solidarity.

Society—The ensuing dynamic of supportive relationships fosters the capacity of individuals in that society to withstand adversity. A virtuous circle begins whereby ever-more individuals awaken to the willingness of getting involved in social solutions that benefit others.

As we will see in the next section due to the interrelated nature of individuals whatever happens in one dimension of their being influences the others, internally and outside.

6.5 The POZE Paradigm

The *Purpose for Power* approach that this chapter is about is anchored in the POZE paradigm. Based on the understanding that human existence is a composition of four dimensions (soul, heart, mind and body, expressed as aspirations, emotions, thoughts and sensations), POZE offers a practical philosophy to induce inner harmony, which is a precondition for smooth and fluid interpersonal relations. This results in improved quality of life among individuals, enabling them to participate in their immediate environment (school, work, families), and wider society. POZE proposes a path for individuals to find and pursue meaning in their life, help others do the same and promote social change (Walther, 2020a).

As seen above, individual well-being is the cause and consequence of collective welfare. The improved subjective well-being that derives when an individual's inner dimensions are optimized leads to the optimization of the individual's interactions with others—which contributes to an improvement in the social context which they then participate actively in. This two-sided comprehension is anchored the quest for meaning which lies at the heart of human development (Frankl, 1946) and necessarily involves others.

Cooperation is part of our DNA (Novak, 2016). POZE helps individuals reconnect with this innate part of their nature, guiding them to feel (emotionally), understand (intellectually) and experience (physiologically) that their personal well-being depends on the well-being of others (Wilkinson & Pickett, 2009); and that it derives from their own active commitment to furthering it (Makransky, 2012). To achieve this, POZE works with the brain's inherent mechanisms, to increase awareness of the interaction between intuitive and deliberate components. 'The world makes much less sense than you think. The coherence comes mostly from the way your mind works.' (Kahneman, 2011). Awareness to the way in which we operate is an essential condition of optimizing the outcomes.

POZE offers an alternative to the collective mindset where self-centered behavior is not only accepted by society but instilled from childhood (Borba, 2016) because such a mindset is to the disadvantage of everyone—of those who need help, of those who are able to help, yet do not act accordingly, and of society. Using the brain's evolutionary triggers, POZE nudges the individual toward prosocial behavior, participation that arises from the inside out. Rather than appealing to pity, it stimulates the human part that instinctively wants to join into a cause larger than personalized welfare.

Life's meaning is discovered in three different ways: by creating work or accomplishing tasks and goals; by experiencing something fully or loving someone; by the attitude that one adopts toward unavoidable suffering. A human's ultimate freedom is his or her ability to choose how to respond to any given circumstance, even the most painful ones. Additionally, people can find meaning in their lives by identifying the unique roles that only they can fulfill (Frankl, 1946). Collective resilience derives from individual resilience; which is rooted in the aspiration to meaning, and the choices we make in the pursuit of this purpose; the WHY of our respective lives. Identifying this aspiration unlocks a person's ability to overcome everyday challenges just as much as dramatic events of loss or illness, and to thrive despite them, by proactively taking charge and participate in one's life (Walther, 2020b).

POZE is grounded in the notion that the mind–matter phenomenon is a coin with two sides. Thoughts and emotions arise in the mind, while sensations occur in the body. Any thought or emotion, desire or aversion that arises manifests itself in a physiological form, impacting the sensations that the individual experiences (Goleman, 1995). Thus, by observing our sensations, we are in fact observing mental activity, facing reality as it is. Over time such attention sharpens awareness to and labeling of emotions; they are no longer abstract and overpowering but become tangible and manageable. Instead of being held captive of our experiences, we can use the body as a tool to identify and master our emotions, and hereby our behavior. We are no longer victim to our instincts.

The present approach sheds a light on individual aspirations as the core of personal empowerment which is the cause and consequence of genuine participation (micro). As we will see people are not only influenced by the communities/institutions (meso), countries (macro) and ultimately the Universe (meta), but influence them in return. Everything is connected. Therefore, individual aspirations are the cornerstones of global prosperity. While acknowledging the impact of macro- and meso-level investments, experiences in Haiti and other locations show why sustainable social change starts with shifts at the micro-level.

The power to shift from passive to proactive attitude, from bystander to participant, applies independently from socioeconomic context and educational status. The following pages lay out the two (intertwined) four-dimensional dynamics that underpin respectively our individual and collective experiences and expressions.

6.6 The Individual Dimensions of Human Existence

How individuals experience their environment and whether they participate in it is influenced by their aspirations, emotions, thoughts and sensations—which are the expression of their soul, heart, mind and body. These four dimensions continuously interact and influence each other, engaged in an ongoing spiral dynamic, from the center to the periphery and from the periphery inward. This internal two-way interaction determines who we are, what we do and how we interact with the outside world.

Starting at the core of our being, the **soul** represents the essence of who we are. It embodies our aspiration, the desire to find meaning in life. Whatever we feel, think and do, is rooted in this craving for a purpose, meaning. The second dimension is our emotions. Schematically and metaphorically speaking, they are in the **heart**, determining how we feel in a situation. Emotions are fundamental in determining attitudes, decisions and actions. No matter how much we 'know' about a certain issue, an emotional impulse will set the trigger that moves our attitude from information, to understanding, to desire for change, to action. The third dimension is the **mind**. Thoughts are the result of an intricate mixture of genetic disposition, education, beliefs, memories, upbringing and environment; they influence an individual's emotions, physical experiences and their behavior; while being influenced

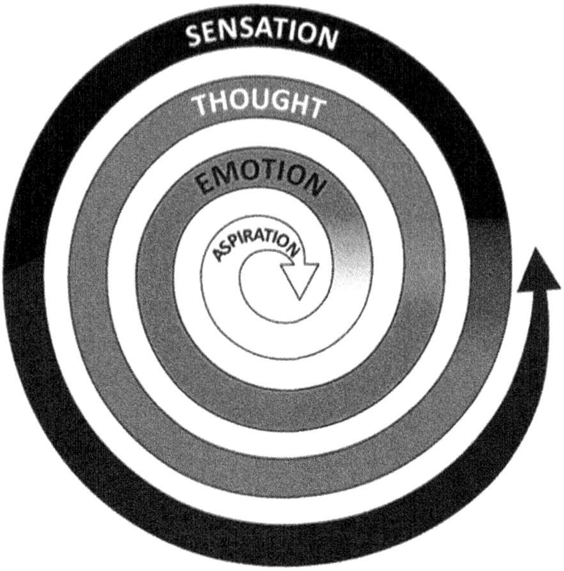

Fig. 6.1 Everything is connected, from the inside out and from the outside in. Our aspirations impact our emotions, which influence our thoughts and hereby our experiences (sensations) and expressions (behavior). Conversely, the way in which we express ourselves causes certain experiences, which result in physical sensations that trigger thoughts and emotions, which fuel or alter our aspirations; and shape our memories. These memories influence our emotions and thoughts in arising situations, and hereby our future expressions and experiences

by them in return. The fourth dimension is the **body**, which is the outer membrane that connects and separates the internal and external realm. As an interface between the inside and the outside, it is the level on which we experience the world, and it is the platform through which we express ourselves in it (Fig. 6.1).

Nothing happens in a vacuum. The body reflects a person's internal circumstances. Conversely, any experience of the environment impacts the inside; shaping their perspective of the world and hereby their reaction to it. Like a stone cast into the water, whatever happens at the center radiates out. Whichever state our internal realm is in impacts our interaction with the outside.

6.7 The Collective Dimensions of Life

The **micro**-dimension refers on the one hand to the four-dimensional internal composition of every individual's being; on the other hand, it denotes the role of the individual in society.

Every person is at the same time part of various **meso**-entities. These meso-entities include different types of communities/institutions, such as a family, church, workplace, school, political party, sports-club, etc. These meso-entities function as an intermediary between the person and the subsequent level. The **macro**-dimension encompasses the economic, political and cultural spheres that individuals and communities evolve in, respectively, and combined these three dimensions form part of the **meta**-dimension, which covers Nature and other aspects of the Universe. It should be noted here that the meta-level includes also supra-national organizations and entities such as the United Nations, due to their global mandate and impact.

Everything is connected. For example, the 'international economy' emanates from human behavior at multiple levels, i.e., an individual migrant (micro) sends remittances back home; an exporting company (meso) sells its wares across borders to another company; a government (macro) sends a grant, i.e., ODA, to finance development programs in another country. Each type of behavior happens in a different collective dimension, depending on the actor behind it; the complementary effect affects the whole and each part.

Every individual is, willingly or not, simultaneously part of several meso- and macro-dimensions and the overall meta-dimension (Fig. 6.2). While the meso-dimension is sub-national, certain institutions at the meso-level have counterparts at supra-national level (i.e., churches, multinational companies). This double

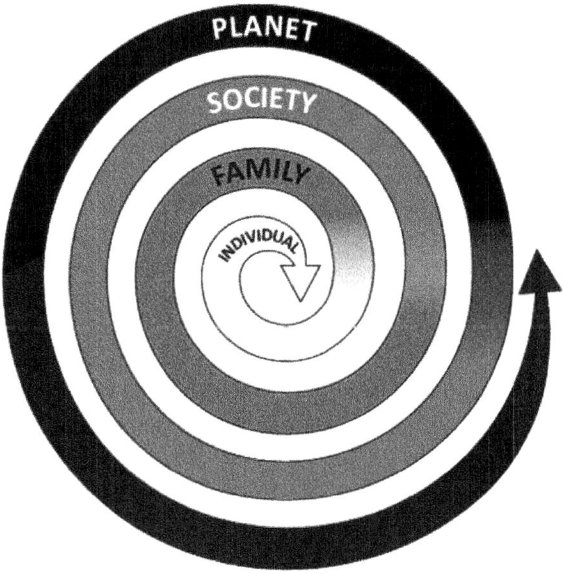

Fig. 6.2 Everything is connected, from the inside out and from the outside in. Individuals represent the micro dimension of a multidimensional system. They form, shape and experience the meso-level via the communities they are part of. The contours of economic, political and cultural systems form the macro-level. Micro-, meso- and macro-dimensions operate within a meta-system that comprises both the interface across these levels as well as between humans and nature. Within a seamless continuum, one dimension is influenced by the others and influences them in turn

nature illustrates the inseparable interaction of and across dimensions. A similar double-sized nature marks the meta-dimension which entails on the one hand supra-national institutions such as the United Nations, and on the other hand the sum total of all entities, their connections, and spheres that are not human-related such as Nature. Since individuals (micro) and local institutions (meso) shape the macro-dimension, and are major components of the meta-dimension, our post-pandemic society hinges on the course that these multiple dimensions of our existence take.

Micro-, meso-, macro- and meta-dimensions mutually influence and shape each other. Whatever happens in one dimension has repercussions within and upon the others. Immediately or eventually, directly or indirectly.

6.8 Participation—Purpose for Power (P4P)

The aim of *Purpose for Power* is not to make solidarity 'fashionable' but normal. Rather than requesting individuals to do one thing or another, the goal is to make them *want* to be part of a social cause. P4P guides young people toward gradual autonomy, with a sense of identity and hope that is built on the understanding of connections—the internal connections that influence who they are and become, and the external connection between their personal well-being and the action that they take for the well-being of others.

Pursuing a logical sequence from Purpose to Passion to Power (which are explained below) P4P gives individuals tools to identify their personal aspirations and pursue their purpose in life. Finding their passion and the place in society where it matters unlocks their innate power—to change themselves, and to influence the circumstances that harm them. P4P addresses individual mindsets because intentions are the precursor of behavior; and behavior is both cause and consequence of the prevailing social unease. To build a World where everyone has a fair chance to high quality of life, we must address the root causes underpinning the material manifestations that prevent many people from reaching their potential.

Purpose—Passion—Power

Purpose in the present context refers to the quest for meaning that is inherent to human nature. The search for an answer to the universal question that an individual needs to ask and answer—Why am I here? *Passion* relates to the emotional investment into our life and living. It arises once we feel that our energy flows in line with our purpose. *Power* derives when this flow is liberated. In the perspective of POZE, it is attached to material assets nor social influence, though the latter may derive from it; rather, it relates to the attitude of choice, or the aspirational and emotional perception that arises when an individual steps out of a bystander position in life into a place of participation. This step is taken inside ourselves, to manifest outside (in interaction with other members of communities and societies).

Change happens from the inside out. It is nurtured from the outside in:

Change from the Inside Out
Society mirrors individuals and vice versa. Because behavior is the physical manifestation of intentions (Levitis et al., 2009), and intentions are micro-representations of the individual's central aspiration to a fulfilled life. The intrinsic quest for meaning is the central driver of human existence. Addressing this quest for meaning is an essential factor of subjective well-being (Frankl, 1946). The form that this aspiration takes in the individual results from education, current context and past experiences (Seligman, 1991). Together with the individual's physiological makeup, which includes the brain's hardware and its interaction with other parts of the body, including both visible ones like the skin, and invisible ones such as hormones and the microbiome (Brody, 2017), this aspiration drives behavior consciously and subconsciously.

Intentions drive decisions, which are the result of an interplay between two kinds of cognitive processes: an automatic intuitive system and an effortful rational system (Tversky & Kahneman, 1982). Nurturing a community that is characterized by compassion and respect begins with its constituents. Awareness of emotions and sensations increases resilience to stress, creates a sense of self-sufficiency, and develops personal leadership (Tang et al., 2015). Indeed, living a 'meaningful life' involves using one's signature strengths in the service of something larger than oneself (Seligman, 2002). This is the main characteristic that distinguishes emotionally resilient individuals from the average.

Like a seed brings fruits, the mindset of individuals results in behavior that influence their social network. Due to so-called emotional contagion, every individual's emotions and behavior trigger similar emotions and behaviors in other people and broader groups (Hatfield et al., 1992) both directly in their immediate environment and indirectly by spreading their state of mind via the social networks they operate in (Carter, 2012). Neuroscience suggests that addressing the decision-making process itself is key to breaking habits, including addiction (Bergland, 2014). The same principle that applies to weakening existing behavior patterns applies to establishing new ones. Action is merely the last piece of a long chain. It manifests an inner situation. Thus, lasting behavioral change requires the systematic identification, targeting and transformation of the (invisible) underlying factors. Changed behavior derives from modifications at the cognitive and emotional levels because these factors underpin the decision-making process. Simultaneously to internal transformation, change can be nurtured at the physical level.

Change from the Outside In
The traditionally assumed logical sequence—think, then act—is often reversed in a personal change process. Paradoxically, we only increase our self-knowledge in the process of making changes to our current course of action (Ibarra, 2015). Priming new habits can begin with actions that are performed consciously, even if the underlying motivation is not intuitive. Gradually, the resulting experiences will result in new habit patterns in the mind. Thinking and introspection may follow physical experimentation—not only vice versa. Transformation involves action,

which is likely to cause discomfort if the intended change requires individuals to move out of their comfort zone. Personal change occurs beyond that zone. Yet when the unfamiliar behavior is performed repeatedly, it gradually induces changes in the physical brain circuitry (Doidge, 2007). Neuroplasticity renders them ever-more permanent until they feel 'normal'. The comfort zone expands.

Social norms derive from the repeated behavior of people. They are the unwritten rules of behavior considered acceptable in a group or Society; resulting from the interplay between beliefs and behavior, between individuals and larger communities (Bicchieri, 2008). These norms are kept in place by the beliefs that underpin them; while nurturing and confirming these beliefs through direct experience (individuals act in line with the belief) and indirect experience (individuals witness other act in line with the belief and to conform they follow). In the same way that poverty and violence, indifference and inequity are condoned as normal circumstances in some parts of the World, avoiding and addressing these issues proactively can become a new norm. Changes of collective belief systems begin with the transformation of individual behavior.

Humans are hardwired to cooperate, and whatever one does for others has benefits in both directions (for the one who acts and the one who's acted for) and beyond. Benefits of prosocial action occur on four levels: i) The very act of giving back to the community boosts a person's happiness, health and sense of physical well-being (Plante, 2012); ii) benefits derive for the one who benefits from the action; iii) beyond this pair of giver/receiver, others who witness acts of kindness experience renewed hope, appeasement and the desire to take similar action (Ramey, 2016); iv) society benefits from an atmosphere of compassion and care among individuals, as the occurrence and acceptability of inequality and deprivation shrink.

POZE changes the perception of the self which affects behavior. Using the continued feedback-loop that connects mind and matter, brain and body (Korb, 2015), it builds a holistic connection on four levels. It,

1. *Connects individuals with their own resources*, by providing them with practical tools to identify, use and nurture their inner assets. The four dimensions mentioned above are involved in this stage of connection: The Soul, by identifying one's purpose. The Heart, by working with one's emotions rather than against them, combining gratitude practices and compassion meditation. The Mind, by training the ability for honest self-inquiry to identify one's present status and the desired destination; this includes the definition of measurable indicators to monitor progress on the way from one to the other. The Body, by learning from experiences, based on enhanced awareness of one's physical experiences and expressions; this is helped by an improved mind–body interplay due to conscious movement and wholesome practices. The parallel pursuit of these four areas results in gradual harmonization, within each dimension and between them. Once inner synchronization is established, individuals gravitate naturally toward the compassionate behavior that is part of their genetic programming.

2. *Connects individuals with their purpose.* Everyone has a unique combination of skills and assets, relationships and experiences. This equips them to fulfill a mission that no one else can tackle in the same way. Identifying, choosing, shaping and pursuing the mission unchains the power that is innate to human nature; which is the core of Empowerment.
3. *Connects individuals to each other*, by building bridges that are grounded in renewed respect for oneself and others. Participants learn compassion for their own journey and for the journeys of others.
4. *Connects individuals with Society*, by empowering them to stand-up for themselves and for the needs of others. As participants understand their own power as 'agents of change', they grow the confidence to take a proactive stance in the events that shape their life and their environment. Feeling harmony on the inside, they experience harmony outside, gaining the ability to experience and express compassion.

An education that is geared toward participation is a critical aspect of life quality because it can open the door to unleash aspiration, feeling, understanding and conscious action. Only if it addresses these four aspects, it enables young people to actively participate in their community, which is central to subjective well-being and collective prosperity. However, in many countries, particularly in the poorer areas, education is based on a traditional top-down model. This form of public education, developed in the 1800s, primarily seeks to inculcate passive knowledge. Trained in such a manner, students tend to grow into citizens without critical questioning skills or an aspirational anchor.

For education to be effective and engaging, it must be designed and delivered in the perspective of genuine participation. Guide children and adolescents to question their environment and come up with solutions to the challenges they notice. Education can shepherd young people toward a life of purpose—by making them understand the impact that their aspirations, emotions, thoughts and sensations have on each other, on themselves and on their community. Attitudes precede action. To be meaningful, participation must be the manifestation of an internal attitude of purpose.

6.9 Approach

The prevailing social environment reflects an individuals' inner state of mind, and it affects it. Thus, it is not enough to cure symptoms. Efforts need to concentrate on the root causes that precede them. To bring about social change, we must address the aspirations of individuals as the precursor of behavior, which is both cause and consequence of the toxic stress which underlies other social problems.

Social destruction often starts in childhood as the brain of the child is sensitive to the smallest influences in their environment (Soleimanpour et al., 2017). Because of this, the enduring effects of toxic stress on children impairs academic achievement, as well as both physical and mental health later in life. Adverse childhood experiences (ACEs) include physical or emotional neglect or both, abuse, poverty, malnutrition and traumatic experiences (Pearce et al., 2019). They can have long-lasting negative consequences. Adverse experiences in childhood can affect the structural and functional development of the brain, giving structural and functional abnormalities in later life, and in adulthood (Herzog & Schmahl, 2018). Repeated adverse childhood experiences can result in a heightened level of stress known as toxic stress (Pearce et al., 2019). ACE are a classic illustration of the mutual influence of brain and body, of experiences and expressions. When children are chronically exposed to stressful events, their neurological development can be disrupted. As a result, the child's cognitive functioning or ability to cope with negative or disruptive emotions may be impaired. Over time, the child may adopt various harmful coping strategies that can contribute to later disease and disability (D'Andrea et al., 2012). Childhood adversity is also associated with an increased risk for developing severe mental illnesses, including schizophrenia, and it has been suggested that it could contribute to some features of the illness, including cognitive impairment.

Toxic stress responses occur when a child experiences strong, frequent and/or prolonged adversity—such as physical or emotional abuse, chronic neglect, caregiver substance abuse or mental illness, exposure to violence and/or the accumulated burdens of family economic hardship—without adequate adult support. All of these derive from active or passive behavior of individuals whose own state of mind has repercussions on others (Harvard Center for the Developing Child, 2020).

Family stressors, such as poverty, elevate the risk. While representing a time bomb that is set-off in early childhood, toxic stress also has a direct impact on adults. Exposure to adversity causes physiological, mental and emotional distress which impact individuals' relationships. Being fractured inside, they unconsciously create a fractured environment (Harvard Center for the Developing Child, 2020). A vicious cycle, when it comes to caregivers and leaders whose inner state of mind determines the imprint on those who depend on them.

The proposed *Purpose for Power* methodology enables individuals to step out of that cycle, for their own benefit, and to the advantage of others. Using a modular and participatory approach that draws on local resources, it is applicable in any context. A combination of positive psychology, mindfulness and stress management techniques is combined with personal leadership and group animation skills, which makes it useful for a wide audience. While pertinent to everyone, primary audiences are caregivers, humanitarian frontline workers and leaders who learn (by doing) how to participate and to help others to be empowered to participate. This is due to the ripple effect that their personal state of mind has on others.

Taking the well-being of caregivers and teachers as an entry-point to build up the well-being of children and adolescents *Purpose for Power* invests in genuine empowerment from the bottom up. Rolled out in stages that build onto each other the training combines theory and praxis. To make the participants understand, feel and practice the framework combines fresh knowledge and exercises that pull people out of their acquired mental space by applying this knowledge onto their own personal journey. An internal and external alignment is systematically nurtured by addressing the twice four connections mentioned above. Being highly interactive and participative, the combination of classroom learning, self-reflection, design thinking, coaching on the job and peer-to-peer support leads to the organic establishment of a network of likeminded practitioners that expands with every person who is trained. In school settings and similar child-focused contexts, there should also be spaces and opportunities (besides classes) in which children participate and have their opinions seriously considered (including child-initiated activities and projects) (Hart, 1992, 2008; Iltus & Hart, 1994).

Based on POZE, P4P participants go through four stages or phases: Learn—Experience—Design—Share, which offers them a different Perspective of themselves and others, that gradually leads to the Optimization of their internal and external setup, which is necessary to access the best version of themselves, their personal Zenith, and to Exposure of that self to the world. Genuine participation ensues. The timing and length of these phases are flexible, depending on the prevailing context and requirements. The intention is a light low-cost implementation process that is conducive to scale and sustainability.

An overview:

Phase 1: **P**erspective (What)—Learn about POZE and the universal principles that underpin it (Mind).

– The philosophy and logic of POZE are explained as a foundation of the practical exercises and the overall P4P methodology. With flexibility to local requirements, add-on topics commonly include emotional intelligence, personal leadership, emotional resilience, self-esteem, positive affirmations, stress management technics including psychological first aid tools to cope with traumatic experiences including post-traumatic stress disorder, and the biological and social setup of adolescents.

Phase 2: **O**ptimization (How)—Experience the underpinning logic first-hand as a tool to rediscover life (Soul).

- Participants acquire the practical skills to share the methodology with their peers and those in their care. The focus is on group management and presentation skills.

Phase 3: **Z**enith (Coaching on the job)—Design a curriculum to help their audiences, while helping themselves move toward their best self (Heart)

- Participants develop modules for their target audience with hands-on professional guidance from the master-trainer, while starting to apply the acquired theory the context of their environment.

Phase 4: **E**xposure (Peer-to-peer support)—Share their curriculum with course peers for feedback and refinement, before its integration in their workspace (Body).

- Coaching by experts is replaced by the mutual support of the participants, who integrate a circle of practitioners who apply a similar holistic perspective.

Purpose for Power is geared toward a balance of now and later. It seeks an immediate impact on the well-being of participants and on the individuals who they interact with. In the case of teachers and caregivers, these benefits extend to children and young people. In the short-term, the latter benefit from the changed attitude and skillset of their mentors; in the medium and long terms, their exposure to role models in the form of these mentors inspires them to shift from passive to active, from bystander to participant in their life and community:

Benefits are individual and collective, direct and indirect immediate and long term:

Among individuals P4P increases the ability and skills to cope with everyday stress and external shocks. Both parties, those who care for and those who are being cared for, benefit.

Among caregivers and teachers, it i) fosters emotional intelligence and stress management capacities, ii) while contributing toward interdisciplinary thinking and multisector working, based on a holistic understanding of factors that shape subjective and collective well-being.

Among youth, it iii) serves to nurture their innate ability to withstand challenges, while iv) empowering them to choose their role in society hereby contributing to their evolution toward engaged citizenship.

At the community level P4P gradually grows a support network to offer youth medium- and long-term coaching; while expanding the range of positive role models they can look toward. A multisector platform of likeminded individuals arises—which contributes to a systemic shift in the siloed modus operandi of many development and education institutions.

Brought to scale, the P4P logic has the potential to induce a new understanding of the young person, as holistic being with aspirations, emotions, sensations and thoughts—four components that must be addressed in a comprehensive manner, not as a fragmented checklist. As a growing number of adults who work with youth adopt a new attitude a shift occurs from the traditional top-down approach to a coaching relationship that nurtures the young person to explore their own potential.

Encountering 'role models' whose values, words and actions are aligned, youth come to understand the link of personal aspirations/civic responsibility that manifests as proactive participation, and of personal well-being/collective well-being.

Every child can become an adult who participates to makes the world a better place. To fulfill this potential, they must grow up with exposure to an environment where compassion and altruism are valued. Research has shown conclusively that childhood experiences shape a person's attitude and action. Children who have compassionate parents tend to be more altruistic (Oliner, 1988); and those who grow up securely attached to their parents behave in a more sympathetic, compassionate way toward their peers (Waters et al., 1979). Children whose parents use inductive corrections that seek understanding rather than punishment are more emphatic (Eisenberg et al., 2010) In contrast, abusive parents who resort to physical violence have less empathetic children (Main & George, 1979).

While the immediate benefits of the approach are enhanced well-being and reduced use of negative coping mechanisms among young people (i.e., over18 years of age); in the long run the subjective well-being that is fostered at their level leads to a changed relationship with their peers and their environment.

As they gradually find peace inside themselves, they increasingly adopt a prosocial attitude toward others. As the understanding arises that their personal well-being depends on the well-being of others (Wilkinson & Pickett, 2009), and that it derives from acting to the benefit of others (Makransky, 2012) the participants become motivated to get involved in their communities. In the long-term perspective, the project plants the seeds of authentic citizenship education.

Underneath superficial differences, all humans share a common moral blueprint (Graham et al., 2013). Five universally available, but variably developed, sets of moral intuitions have been distilled by researchers: (avoid/prevent) Harm/care, Fairness/reciprocity, In-group/loyalty, Authority/respect and Purity/sanctity. (Graham et al., 2011; Haidt, 2013). POZE builds on commonalities, with agility to integrate the prevailing culture. That localized logic makes P4P relatable and applicable with audiences everywhere.

Having established the premises of the approach, we will now investigate the objectives and actions that shaped the pilot project that was conducted in Port-au-Prince in 2017/2018.

6.9.1 Country Focus Haiti

Haiti was chosen to start rolling-out POZE in the form of *Purpose for Power* because the country has all the ingredients to thrive yet remains paralyzed due to lacking investment in the minds and hearts of young people.

Note—Data in this section comes from the Institut Haïtien de Statistique et d'Informatique, Enquête sur les Conditions de Vie des Ménages Après Séisme (2012); United Nations Children's Fund, The State of the World's Children 2019; Centers for Disease Control and Prevention, Violence Against Children Survey 2012; Pan American Health Organization/World Health Organization 2019.

Close to half (42%) of the 11-million population is under 18 years of age. While the total fertility rate has been declining, the population is expected to reach 13.1 million by 2031. 52% of the population live in urban areas, with 24% of the Haitian population living in the capital Port-au-Prince.

It is a low-income country, with a gross domestic product per capita of almost $1,700, and it ranked 163 out of 188 countries in the 2015 Human Development Index. Nearly 70 per cent of all children under 5 years of age live in monetary poor households. Children, including adolescents (10–18 years old), are severely affected by multidimensional poverty. In urban areas, 82 per cent of children experience at least one deprivation of their basic needs, while in rural areas, the rate reaches 97 per cent (IHSI 2012). The main causes for the lack of access to basic services are financial constraints within families, social inequality, the limited capacity of public institutions and insufficient public social expenditure. The geographic location of Haiti puts it at risk to natural disasters and the negative impacts of climate change; including earthquakes, hurricanes, floods and droughts. Over the past decade, the impact of Hurricane Matthew (2016), a cholera outbreak (2010) and an Earthquake of 7.2 magnitude (2020) demonstrated the lingering vulnerability of the country and its population to disaster.

The causes and consequences of Adverse Childhood Experiences (ACE) have been documented in Haiti since 2016, including their long-term impact on economic development. Exposure to violence and abuse, including corporal punishment and gender-based violence, is a substantial problem. One in four women and one in five men are victims of sexual abuse before 18 years of age. Eighty-five per cent of children 2 to 14 years of age are victims of violent discipline at home, 79 per cent are victims of corporal punishment and 16 per cent suffer from extreme corporal punishment. One in four children live separately from their parents. Over 700 unregulated residential care facilities operate in the country, hosting an estimated 30,000 children, 80 per cent of whom are not orphans. The prevalence of HIV/AIDS among the population has remained stable at 2.2 per cent since 2006 (WHO, 2017). Girls and young women are the most affected, with a rate of 2.7 per cent against 1.7 per cent for boys and young men. (WHO, 2017). But although almost all adolescents have heard of HIV/AIDS, only around one-third have comprehensive knowledge of how to protect themselves.

Haiti is one country among many to illustrate the gap between legal commitments to human rights, and the reality experienced by those who are meant to benefit from the resulting entitlements. It signed the Convention of the Rights of the Child's (CRC/1995) but has not established an operational interministerial committee related to the CRC's implementation. It also ratified the Convention on the Elimination of All Forms of Discrimination against Women (CEDAW/1981), International Convention on the Elimination of All Forms of Racial Discrimination (CCPR/1991); International Covenant on Economic, Social and Cultural Rights (CESCR/2013), Convention on the Rights of Persons with Disabilities (CRPD/2019) and the Optional Protocol to the Convention on the Rights of the Child on the sale of children child prostitution and child pornography (CRC-OP-SC/2014) (OHCHR Retrieved October 2020).

Haiti has articulated its long-term vision in the 'Strategic Plan for the Development of Haiti', ambitioning to turn into an emerging country by 2030, with an emphasis on improved access to health and education. The government committed to establish a national system that offers a protective environment for children. Despite significant progress, much remains to be done to align reality and the range of pledges that the country made in the form of international conventions, the Millennium Development Goal (MDG) and the Sustainable Development Goal (SDG) Declarations. Aspirations and actions are mostly disparate thus far, and despite overall improvements progress has been slow and distributed unequally.

Deep inequities and exclusion persist deriving from location and socioeconomic status: Only 66 per cent of children from the poorest households attend primary school against 92 per cent from the richest. 80 per cent of schools are privately run, on a fee-based system. Of children who drop out of primary school, 8 out of 10 were overage because they entered school late or had to repeat several grades.

Compliance with authority is the underlying current of Haiti's social establishment; it is cultivated early. Following a unilateral education model, schools push out information that is supposed to be accepted, unchallenged. Parents raise their children in the same dynamic. This context is not favorable to the emergence and growth of critical minds; nor does it nurture individuals who participate in society. Unless people learn from an early age to think for themselves, they are an easy prey for those who know what they want, which is often the case of offspring from the upper quintiles. The latter tend to send their children out of the country to study. While often the latter do not return if they do, they are better equipped to face the harsh reality of their country (Jadotte, 2012).

Children learn what they are taught and emulate what they experience. Lasting change requires an environment where solution-seeking is the norm, and where collective approaches are in everyone's interest. Starting in primary school children must be exposed to the four core questions that drive their existence (Why am I here? Who am I? Where do I want to be? And What can I do to align my aspirations and my actions). They must seek their own answers rather than adopting those of others.

Dedicating time to identifying one's purpose may appear like luxury when millions lack the basics of survival. Yet, it is the only empowerment that lasts and a step that can be undertaken by everyone, everywhere, for free. Provided they are conscious of the possibility. P4P was set up as a program to train teachers and caregivers to practice a radically different type of teaching. Starting with a prototype at the onset of 2017, which was implemented within a partnership of UNICEF and 25 non-governmental organizations, P4P has proven to be adaptable to diversified audiences, across generations. Following a methodology based on long-term research and data from psychological, physiological and social disciplines, the curricula of the prototype's training of trainers was developed in collaboration with two Haitian-based institutions to ensure it was appropriate to local Haitian culture.

Participants of the inception phase were selected from local NGOs working on education and on preventing abuse, neglect, exploitation, and violence against children. These NGOs work with marginalized adolescents in Port-au-Prince and the Grand Anse department. Selection criteria included on the one hand a strong commitment of the candidate to invest time and energy, their proven social engagement and daily hands-on work with adolescents; on the other it was required from the emitting agency that the participant would have leeway to use their new knowledge and skills upon return to their workplace. To assess the process, progress and results of the P4P approach—assessments were conducted before the course and before each section; additional monitoring occurred during implementation of each segment and an evaluation afterward. To get an understanding of the actual impact of the training on the adolescents the participants work with, quantitative data were combined with qualitative data collected by the means of testimonials.

The results of the project are direct and indirect, immediate and long term. Direct immediate benefits reside with the trained caregivers; indirect benefits pertain to the adolescents they work with. In terms of direct long-term outcome, it was expected that the project would contribute to a new understanding of adolescence, and according program evolution. Long-term monitoring is required to prove this, and not enough time has elapsed yet.

Outputs as reflected by an external assessment done six months after the completion of the training showed the following. By March 2018 (i.e., in about a year),

- Key NGO implementation partners of UNICEF Haiti's Education and Child Protection programs had at least one animator trained in the new methodology. He/she acted as a role model who inspired his/her peers, and the adolescents he/she works with, due to his/her attitude and action. He/she is equipped with the skills and tools necessary to accompany adolescents in high-risk settings on their journey toward engaged citizenship.
- 50 percent of the teenagers who had been coached by the trained social workers had been familiarized with the concept of stress management. They started to uncover their own resources and were able to use them to face to cope with challenges in a positive manner.
- A platform of organizations involved in youth support had been initiated, including both international and Haitian non-governmental organizations. These institutions attributed attention to positive stress management and personal leadership. The continued exchange and networking within this network contribute to increased understanding of adolescent well-being and care in the Haitian development and humanitarian sector.

The post-training assessment conclusively showed that the training equipped the participating caregivers with a new self-understanding and tools to nurture and share this stronger self in the relationship with others. Deriving from their boosted self-awareness and confidence they turned into role-models for those in their care, who became more confident, proactive and resilient to stress themselves. To get an understanding of longer-term changes and sustainability assessments should be conducted at regular intervals.

6.9.2 Conclusions and Perspective

One may argue that not enough time has elapsed to prove outcomes, that one country is not enough to show universal applicability and that a large-scale training of trainers' approach would be costly to implement and difficult to measure. These arguments are valid. However, human beings evolve over time. Infrastructure, be it a school building, a waterpoint or a health center that is built in one year may be broken shortly after. It was measurable yet not sustainable. Food that is distributed one day will be gone the next day. Unless distribution is continued, the person will be hungry again. Yet education that is conceived in the perspective of equipping the young person with tools to identify, nurture and multiply their own innate resources is a gift for life. Because it empowers the person to participate in their own life and to make a difference in the life of others.

The alignment of an individual's aspirations and actions leads to internal alignment, which conditions individual well-being and social harmony. Whereas individual well-being is the cause and consequence of collective welfare, social harmony is essential to make collective welfare last. Both depend on optimizing the twice four dimensions the influence who we are and become, individually and collectively.

Once an individual's inner dimensions are aligned their interaction with others improves. Identifying and pursuing their purpose enables people to participate within their communities, countries and thus to be a proactive part of the Universe that we are all part of. Participative education models can nurture such internal and intrapersonal harmonization.

To mature (individually) and maintain (social) well-being, material and immaterial factors are required. This endeavor is not achieved with short-term fixes that focus on one side of the equation, the 'hardware' of material development. Building a society where everyone has a fair chance identify and reveal their potential, which is the cause and condition of genuine participation requires vision and commitment. Such a conducive social setting can be nurtured from the bottom up and from the top down. It must be pursued with the ambition of interconnected communities that lift individuals to fulfill their potential and galvanized in the understanding of the ongoing interplay between individuals and society. The latter may be an incentive for all stakeholders, including those in formal power positions, to not only acknowledge that social change is needed, but act accordingly.

An individual and collective mindset that enables the participation of all is the starting point of a Society that is conducive to the fulfillment of its potential. Because the latter is the cause and condition of individual fulfillment. Both must be conceived with a holistic understanding of the interplay between individuals, communities, countries and ultimately the Planet. The smallest common denominator—the aspiration of individuals for meaning—is the starting point of this gigantic task. It is what *Purpose for Power* contributes to. We must shape society based on the premise that genuine participation is not a possibility, but indispensable for inclusive quality of life.

References

Anand, P. (2016). *Happiness Explained*. Oxford University Press.

Barile, J. P., Reeve, B. B., Smith, A. W., Zack, M. M., Mitchell, S. A., Kobau, R., Cella, D. F., Luncheon, C., & Thompson, W. W. (2013). Monitoring population health for healthy people 2020: Evaluation of the NIH PROMIS Global Health, CDC healthy days, and satisfaction with life instruments. *Quality of Life Research: An International Journal of Quality of Life Aspects of Treatment, Care and Rehabilitation, 22*(6), 1201–1211. https://doi.org/10.1007/s11136-012-0246-z.

Bicchieri, C. (2008). *Norms in the Wild. How to Diagnose, Measure, and Change Social Norms.* Oxford University Press.
Borba, M. (2016). *Unselfie. Why Empathetic kids succeed in our All-about-me-world.* Australian Book Company.
Broderick, J. E., & Schwartz, S. (2008). Lottery winners and accident victims: Is happiness relative? *Journal of Personality and Social Psychology, 36*(8), 917–927. https://doi.org/10.1037/0022-3514.36.8.917.
Brody, J. E. (2017). *Unlocking the Secrets of the Microbiome.* Retrieved from https://www.nytimes.com/2017/11/06/well/live/unlocking-the-secrets-of-the-microbiome.html.
Campie, P. E., Paktis, A., Flynn, K., & McDermott, K. (2015). Developing a coherent approach to youth well-being in the fields of child welfare, juvenile justice, education, and health: A systematic literature review. *Families in Society, 96*(3), 175–184. https://doi.org/10.1606/1044-3894.2015.96.22.
Carter, B. (2012). *Children's well-being: Priorities and considerations.* First Published 2012, June 18; https://doi.org/10.1177/1367493512451061.
Centers for Disease Control and Prevention. (CDC). (2012). *Violence Against Children Survey 2012.* Haiti.
Chen, S., & Bonanno, G. A. (2020). Psychological adjustment during the global outbreak of COVID-19: A resilience perspective. *Psychological Trauma: Theory, Research, Practice, and Policy, 12*(S1), S51.
D'Andrea, W., Solbach, B, Ford, J., Spinazzola, J., & Kolk van der, B. A. (2012). Understanding Interpersonal Trauma in Children: Why We Need a Developmentally Appropriate Trauma Diagnosis. *American Orthopsychiatric Association 2012, 82*(2), 187–200. https://doi.org/10.1111/j.1939-0025.2012.01154.x.
Dewey, J. (1938). *Experience & Education.* Kappa Delta Pi.
Diener, E., Emmons, R. A., Larsen, R. J., & Griffin, S. (1985). The satisfaction with life scale. *Journal of Personality Assessment., 1985*(49), 71–75. https://doi.org/10.1207/s15327752jpa4901_13.
Doidge, N. (2007). *The brain that changes itself: Stories of personal triumph from the frontiers of brain science.* Viking Press.
Eisenberg, N. Fabes, R, Hoffman, M. (1. December 2010) Interaction of Affect and Cognition in Empathy. *Society Issues Policy Review, 4*(1), 143–180. https://doi.org/10.1111/j.1751-2409.2010.01020.x.
Fayers, P. M., & Machin, D. (2007). *Quality of life: The assessment, analysis and interpretation of patient-reported outcomes.* Wiley.
Frankl, V. (1946). *Man's search for meaning.* Beacon.
Frankl, V. E. (1946). *Man's search for meaning.* Simon and Schuster. (Republished 1985).
Freire, P. (2006). *Pedagogy of the oppressed, 30th Anniversary.* Continuum. 1970.
Goleman, D. (1995). *Emotional Intelligence.* Bantam Books.
Graham, J., Haidt, J., Koleva, S., Motyl, M., Iyer, R., Wojcik, S., & Ditto, P. H. (2013). Moral Foundations Theory: The pragmatic validity of moral pluralism (PDF). *Advances in Experimental Social Psychology., 47*, 55–130. https://doi.org/10.1016/b978-0-12-407236-7.00002-4.ISBN9780124072367.
Graham, J., Nosek, B. A., Haidt, J., Iyer, R., Koleva, S., & Ditto, P. H. (2011). Mapping the moral domain. *Journal of Personality and Social Psychology, 101*(2), 366–385. https://doi.org/10.1037/a0021847.
Guyer, P., & Horstmann, R.-P. (2015). Idealism. In E. N. Zalta (ed.), *The Stanford encyclopedia of philosophy* (Fall 2015 ed.). Retrieved from http://plato.stanford.edu/archives/fall2015/entries/idealism/.
Haidt, J. (2013) *The righteous mind: Why good people are divided by politics and religion.* Random House.
Hagerty, M., Cummings, R., Ferris, A., Land, K., Michalos, A., et al. (2001). Quality of life indexes for national policy: Review and agenda for research. *Social Indicators Research, 55*, 1–96. https://doi.org/10.1023/A:1010811312332.

Hatfield, E, Cacioppo, J., & Rapson, R. (1992). Primitive emotional contagion. *Review of Personality and Social Psychology, 14*. 151–177.

Hart, R. (1992) Children's Participation: From Tokenism to Citizenship. UNICEF Innocenti Essays, No. 4, Florence, Italy: International Child Development Centre of UNICEF.

Hart R. (2008) Stepping Back from 'The Ladder': Reflections on a Model of Participatory Work with Children. In A. Reid, B. B. Jensen, J. Nikel, & V. Simovska (eds.), *Participation and Learning*. Springer.

Harvard Center of the Developing Child. (2020). *Connecting the Brain to the Rest of the Body: Early Childhood Development and Lifelong Health Are Deeply Intertwined*, Working Paper No. 15. Retrieved (Sept 2020) https://www.developingchild.harvard.edu.

Herzog, J. I., & Schmahl, C. (2018). Adverse Childhood Experiences and the Consequences on Neurobiological, Psychosocial, and Somatic Conditions Across the Lifespan. *Frontiers in psychiatry, 9*, 420. https://doi.org/10.3389/fpsyt.2018.00420.

Howell, K. H., Coffey, J. K., Fosco, G. M., Kracke, K., Nelson, S. K., Rothman, E. F., et al. (2016). Seven reasons to invest in well-being. *Psychology of Violence, 6*(1), 8–14. https://doi.org/10.1037/vio0000019.

Hudson, J. M., & Bruckman, A. S. (2004). The bystander effect: A lens for understanding patterns of participation. *Journal of the Learning Sciences, 13*(2), 165–195. https://doi.org/10.1207/s15327809jls1302_2.

Huppert, F. A., & Baylis, N. (2004). Well-being: towards an integration of psychology, neurobiology and social science. Philosophical transactions of the Royal Society of London. *Series B, Biological sciences, 359*(1449), 1447–1451.

Ibarra, H. (2015). *"Act Like a Leader, Think Like a Leader"*. Harvard Business Review Press.

Iltus, S., & Hart, R. (1994). Participatory planning and design of recreational spaces with children. *Architecture & Comportement/architecture & Behaviour, 10*(4), 361–370.

Institut Haïtien de Statistique et d'Informatique. (2012). *Enquête sur les Conditions de Vie des Ménages Après Séisme.* (Haiti) Port-au-Prince.

Jadotte, E. (2012). *Brain Drain, Brain Circulation and Diaspora Networks in Haiti.* UNCTAD. Background Paper No. 1. https://unctad.org/system/files/non-official-document/ldcr2012-bp1.pdf.

Kahneman, D. (2011). *Thinking fast and slow*. Farrar, Straus & Giroux.

Kaufman, S.B. (2016). The Differences between Happiness and Meaning in Life. Scientific American Blog Network. January 2016. Retrieved June 2021 from https://blogs.scientificamerican.com/beautiful-minds/the-differences-between-happiness-and-meaning-in-life/.

Korb, A. (2015). *Upward Spiral: Using Neuroscience to Reverse the Course of Depression, One Small Change at a Time Paperback.* New Harbinger Publications; 1st edition.

Main, M., & George, C. (1979). Social interactions of young abused children: Approach, avoidance, and aggression. *Child Development, 50*(2), 306–318. https://doi.org/10.2307/1129405.

Makransky, J. (2012). *Compassion in Buddhist Psychology. Compassion and Wisdom in Psychotherapy*. Guilford Press.

Michalos, A.C. (2015). *Ancient views on the quality of life*. Springer. https://doi.org/10.1007/978-3-319-16525-7.

Nolte, T., et al. (2011). Interpersonal stress regulation and the development of anxiety disorders: An attachment-based developmental framework. *Frontiers in Behavioral Neuroscience, 5*(55), 21. https://doi.org/10.3389/fnbeh.2011.00055.

Novak, M. (2016). *Super cooperators. Altruism, evolution, and why we need each other to succeed paperback*. Simon and Schuster.

OHCHR. UN Treaty Body Database. Retrieved (October 2020) from https://tbinternet.ohchr.org/_layouts/15/TreatyBodyExternal/Treaty.aspx?CountryID=74&Lang=EN.

Oliner, S. P., & Oliner, P. M. (1988). *The altruistic personality: rescuers of Jews in Nazi Europe.* The Free Press.

Pearce, A., Dundas, R. Whitehead, M., & Taylor-Robinson, D. (2019). Pathways to inequalities in child health. https://doi.org/10.1136/archdischild-2018-314808.

Plante, T. G. (2012). *Helping others offers surprising benefits*. Psychology Today. Retrieved from https://www.psychologytoday.com/us/blog/do-theright-thing/201207/helping-others-offers-surprising-benefits-0.
Ramey, S. (2016). *There are also benefits to those witnessing acts of kindness*. Retrieved from https://exploringyourmind.com/benefits-witnessing-acts-kindness/.
Rigolon, A. (2011). A space with meaning: Children's involvement in participatory design processes. *Design Principles and Practices, 5*, 1833–1874.
Sanders, J., Munford, R., Thimasarn-Anwar, T., Liebenberg, L., & Ungar, M. (2015). The role of positive youth development practices in building resilience and enhancing wellbeing for at-risk youth. *Child Abuse Neglect, 42*, 40–53. https://doi.org/10.1016/j.chiabu.2015.02.006. Epub: 2015 Mar 12. PMID: 25770347.
Schwartz, S. (2006). Basic human values: Theory, measurement, and applications. *Revue Francaise de Sociologie, 47*, 929–968,977,981.
Seligman, M. E. P. (1991). *Learned optimism: How to change your mind and your life*. Pocket Books.
Seligman, M. E. P. (2002). *Authentic happiness: Using the new positive psychology to realize your potential for lasting fulfillment*. Free Press.
Sirgy, J. (2002). *The Psychology of Quality of Life*, Vol. 12. Springer, ISBN: 978-90-481-6093-8.
Sen, A. (2009). *Capitalism beyond the crisis*. The New York Review of Books.
Sen, A. (2004). Capability and well-being. In M. Nussbaum & A. Sen, (eds.), *The quality of life* (pp. 30–53). Routledge.
Soleimanpour, S, Geierstanger, S, & Brindis, CD. (Sep-Oct 2017). Adverse Childhood Experiences and Resilience: Addressing the Unique Needs of Adolescents. *Acad Pediatr, 17*(7S), 108-S114. https://doi.org/10.1016/j.acap.2017.01.008. PMID: 28865641.
Tang, Y. Y., Hölzel, B. K., & Posner M. I. (2015). The neuroscience of mindfulness meditation. *Nature Reviews Neuroscience, 16*(4), 213–225. https://doi.org/10.1038/nrn3916. Epub: 2015 Mar 18. PMID: 25783612.
Tversky, A., & Kahneman, D. (1982). Judgment under uncertainty: Heuristics and biases. In D. Kahneman, P. Slovic, & A. Tversky, (eds.), *Judgment under uncertainty: Heuristics and biases* (pp. 3–20). Cambridge University Press.
United Nations Children's Fund, (UNICEF) (2019). The State of the World's Children 2019. UN Committee on the Rights of the Child (CRC), General comment No. 12 (2009): The right of the child to be heard, 20 July 2009, CRC/C/GC/12, available at: https://www.refworld.org/docid/4ae562c52.html. (Accessed: 14 June 2021).
Waterman, A. S., Schwartz, S. J., & Conti, R. (2008). The implications of two conceptions of happiness (hedonic enjoyment and eudaimonia) for the understanding of intrinsic motivation. *Journal of Happiness Studies, 9*, 41–79. https://doi.org/10.1007/s10902-006-9020-7.
Walther, C. (2020a). *Development, Humanitarian Aid and Social Welfare. Social Change from the inside Out*. Springer Nature.
Walther, C. (2020b). *Humanitarian Work, Social Change and Human behavior. Compassion for Change*. Springer Nature.
Walther, C. (2020c). *Development and Connection in the times of COVID. Corona's Call for Conscious Choices*, Springer Nature.
Waterman, A. S. (1993). *Two conceptions of happiness: Contrasts of personal expressiveness (eudaimonia) and hedonic enjoyment. Journal of Personality and Social Psychology, 64*(4), 678–691. https://doi.org/10.1037/0022-3514.64.4.678.
Waters, E, Wippman, J, & Sroufe, L. A. (1979 Sep). Attachment, positive affect, and competence in the peer group: two studies in construct validation. *Child development, 50*(3), 821–829. PMID: 498856 Stephanie Tutors (2012).
Wilkinson, R., & Pickett, K. (2009). The spirit level: why more equal societies almost always do better. *London: Allen Lane, Leadership and Policy in Schools, 11*(1), 129–134. https://doi.org/10.1080/15700763.2011.577928.
Wierzbicka, A. (2004). 'Happiness in cross-linguistic & cross-cultural perspective. *Australian National University. Daedalus, 133*, 34–43. https://doi.org/10.1162/001152604323049370..

7 Childhood Geography from the South: The Right to Participation of Children Living in Rural Settings

Claudia Andrea Mikkelsen

7.1 Introduction

South America's rurality brings together peasantry, small and medium-sized producers, large producers, transnational corporations and agribusinesses. They are traditional actors to whom the arrival of urban population integrates. Since the 1990s, rurality started to be seen as an alternative to life and enjoyment of free time. Therefore, rurality establishes as a dispute territory for diverse subjects who are linked in dissimilar ways with the territory. Among all the rural group of actors, it is interesting to look around rural children, to the meaning and significance of inhabiting rural territories from their voices.

The aim of this chapter is to contribute to the debate of rurality expressed in the role of children as subjects with rights based on their opportunities of participation.

Methodologically, the analysis of specialized literature and the review of examples from the Southern Cone are used. Adding from this contribution to the studies of Childhood Geography with a localized thought.

The Childhood Geography (Holloway, 2014) is a recent field of intellectual debate concerning children, young people and adults. Although this field rooted throughout the 1960s–1970s, it significantly grew during the 1990s, especially in the Anglo-Saxon Geography from where the greatest contributions to the study of children's daily lives can be found (Ortiz Guitard, 2007). The turning point that took place around 1990 aims at researching not about children but for and with children. Malatesta and Granados Sanchez (2017, p. 634) express that Childhood Geography considers three thematic units of analysis: the mechanism of

C. A. Mikkelsen (✉)
Instituto de Humanidades y Ciencias Sociales (INHUS)/Consejo Nacional de Investigaciones Científicas (CONICET), Universidad Nacional de Mar del Plata, Mar del Plata, Argentina

G. Tonon (ed.), *Re-defining Children's Participation in the Countries of the South*, Kindheit – Bildung – Erziehung. Philosophische Perspektiven,
https://doi.org/10.1007/978-3-662-64167-5_7

reconstruction of the geography of the everyday; the physical and material characteristics of the places, and the function of the body as the first instrument of space exploration. The Childhood Geography aims to abandon the adult centered vision (Malatesta & Granados Sanchez, 2017) and give boys and girls their voices. This leads researchers to work on the socio-spatial inequalities of children, with overlapping and superimposed presence of children with voices and of others who have been silenced and marginalized.

In recent years, the agenda is expanded with the need to encourage studies on children from Historical Geography, in order to confirm current assumptions about the use of public space, past and present (Karsten, 2005); the public space use differentials that reinforce the privatization of children, a situation from which children become over controlled and over structured by adults (Karsten, 2005). In urban space, considerations revolve around the place of children in cities, public spaces, especially play areas; research on the use of free time and places of enjoyment; community participation in cities; and children's policies. In rural areas, discussions concern about the idyllic view of rurality, participation in rural communities, rural work. Issues to which are added for example the war, violence, education, children's health, among others (Guitart et al., 2012; Ortiz Guitart, 2007; Phillips, 2001).

As is raised in the list of concerns addressed by the Childhood Geography, participation in urban or rural spaces is a question of interest on which this text seeks to contribute.

After this introduction, the text is structured in a conceptual section on rurality and children, followed by a methodological subtitle. Later, the results are presented and, to finish, a series of synthetizing comments.

7.2 Rurality

There is no unequivocal or closed conceptualization about rurality, its meanings vary, as expressed by Gaudin (2019), according to the disciplines of approach, the span of time considered, and the contexts analyzed; this is due to the complexity of the processes present in rural territories. It is interesting to consider that spaces and their inhabitants are not exclusively urban or rural, but often have characteristics of both, because of their multiple interactions (Gaudin, 2019, p. 16).

Since 1990, it is possible to refer to a shift in the way rurality is studied and understood, linked to multi-employment, environmental protection, interaction with urbanity, where the agricultural debate is set aside to focus on the rural debate (Urcola, 2011).

The notion of rurality becomes a territorial category, whose decisive attribute is in the organization of its ecosystems, in a relatively low demographic density, in the sociability of inter-knowledge and in its dependence on cities (Abramovay, 2006, p. 51). In the early 1990s, the concept of a rurality new in the Latin American debate (Llambí Insua & Perez, 2007; Llambi, 2012), which in a critical sense, is postulated as Neoliberal Rurality (Ramírez Miranda, 2011) and is characterized by paying attention to elements that would differentiate rurality in previous periods, linked to the multi-activity or multi-functionality of rural households (Kay, 2016).

Agricultural activity ceases to be the central focus of rural areas, expands the vision from agricultural to rural, emphasizing the multi-functionality of rural areas due to the increasing importance of non-agricultural activities and the more fluid relationship between the rural and the urban, the local and the global, highlighting changes in cultural patterns and rural living (Kay, 2007). Out of this new rurality, there is a territory where different actors live together, with dissimilar interests, enabling the generation of tensions for land uses (González, 2015), and giving visibility to actors such as women, children and older adults. In the face of the context of conceptual diversity mentioned above, it is interesting to reflect on a particular population group, rural children.

7.3 Children's Participation

Placing focus on children allows to give voice to those who are carriers of rights, involves broadening the view by incorporating new social groups, new themes and problems that were absent in geographical studies since they were subsumed in general of the adult population (Baylina et al., 2006).

Childhood was never the same for all children in the world, it is actually a social construct (Valentine, 1996). Childhood is produced and a product of the place and time of birth and residence. The Convention of Children's Rights established that a child is a person up to the age of 18. However, being a child is not the same in every country in the world. Many children still experience gaps between formal rights and effective exercise, depending on the place of birth and residence and the socioeconomic characteristics of their homes.

The debate among social scientists about children has built and rebuilt various stories, sometimes perceiving them as angels, sometimes as demons, in a binary discourse that still persists (Valentine, 2004).

In the middle ages, children were seen same as adults; there were no differences in community life, no differences in issues that could or could not be talked about in front of children (Moreira Lopes & Vasconcellos, 2006). The social, economic, religious and political changes that occurred at the end of the seventeenth century began to explore the appreciation of children, which arises together with the organization of bourgeois society, based on the ideals of liberalism (Moreira Lopes & Vasconcellos, 2006). This is how families began to organize around their children, their care and prominence.

The twentieth century witnessed the emergence of a perception of children as universal, children are innocent, incompetent and vulnerable. Childhood is a happy time, irresponsible and free. This idea contrasts with the time space reality that children live in daily life; therefore, there is no universality in the spatial experience of childhood (Valentine, 2004) but inequalities and injustices. Despite the academic advances made, children live at risk in their daily lives, domestic and peer violence, early institutionalization, disarticulation of families, street life, child labor, sexual exploitation, among other circumstances, which violate the right to a healthy, harmonious development and to a well-being typical of this stage of life (Mieles Barrera & Tonon, 2015).

Being born and living in certain cultural contexts, in more or less developed areas, in urban or rural space, leave traces on the life trajectories of children, in such sense, studying their possibilities of participation attends knowledge in their extension of rights.

In the 1990s, Hart (1993) defined children's participation as the process of sharing decisions, which influences both their lives and the lives of the community in which they live. Years later, Crowley (1998) stated that participation is a key management principle, i.e. a facilitating right since its compliance ensures compliance with other rights. Participation is a basic civil and political right.

Nomura and Solari (2005) recovered what was specified by Save the Children, Sweden, and pointed out that participation is the practice of the power of children to make their opinions be seriously taken into account and to take decisions combined with other issues affecting their lives and those of their community in a responsible manner, according to their degree of maturity and development.

Checkoway (2011, p. 341) considered participation as a field of practice and subject of study which includes initiatives involving young people according to their race, ethnicity, class, gender or other social identity; in education, environment, housing, or other issues; and in rural areas, small towns, suburbs or neighborhoods of cities in nations worldwide.

7.4 Methodology

The research project 'Quality of life of 12 years old children in the Province of Buenos Aires' was developed during 2017–2018 in the Province of Buenos Aires, directed by Dr. Graciela Tonon and included in the LOMASCyT Program of the Universidad Nacional de Lomas de Zamora, Argentina; 690 inquiries were made of children living in different locations in the Province of Buenos Aires; some corresponding to Greater Buenos Aires and others in different localities of the province. In all cases, parents and/or guardians gave authorizations and the staff of educational institutions collaborated. It was a self-managed questionnaire, specifically applied to children attending the first year of secondary education (Tonon et al., 2018). Such questionnaire was originally prepared by the team that coordinated the project *The Children's Worlds*, adjusted to the Argentine case, considering its contextual peculiarities. We refer to ISCWeb, which encompasses different dimensions in reference to children's lives. Each of these dimensions contains closed type questions, multiple-choice questions, quantization questions and Likert scales (attitudes).

From this set of dimensions, questions that approach the concern of this work, which is the right to participate of children in rural settings, are analyzed in this chapter:

- I know the rights that children have.
- I know about the United Nations Convention on the Rights of the Child.
- I think that in my country, adults respect the rights of children.
- In my country, children are allowed to make choices/decisions about their lives.
- My parents and I make together decisions about my life.
- My teachers listen to me and take into account what I say.
- I have opportunities to participate in decisions about things that are important to children.
- How satisfied are you with the freedom you have?
- I am good at managing my daily responsibilities.

This chapter focuses on the results of the General Pueyrredon District (PGP), specifically two public educational institutions that carry out their tasks in rural settings. It is a non-probabilistic sample. The selected schools were chosen from direct contacts with the District Education Headquarters.

General Pueyrredon District, located to the southeast of the province of Buenos Aires amounts to, according to INDEC data for 2010, 618,989 inhabitants, of which 21.5% comprise the group of 0 to 14 years, 64.2% gather the potentially active population, i.e., 15 to 64 years of age, and 14.2% are definitive passive population, i.e., they are over 65 years of age. General Pueyrredon comprises a wide range of activities and services related to tourism, extraction and transformation in relation to primary resources associated with agriculture, livestock, fisheries and horticulture. In its nearby territory, it shows a leadership role over a set of population centers of lower rank and their respective areas of influence, regarding education, health, administration and other services (Mikkelsen et al., 2013). Mar del Plata, head city of this district, is complemented in its territorial organization by a set of cities, minor towns and scattered rural population spaces. Specifically, the analysis of the inquiries refers to schools in the minor towns El Boquerón and Paraje Los Ortiz (Fig. 7.1).

El Boquerón is located alongside route 88 and is situated twenty-three kilometers from the city of Mar del Plata. Uses of this territory are contrasting. The units closest to route 88 correspond to residences, contiguous to them there is a strip of farms, finally ranches and then El Boquerón site. It is demarcated as a center for the provision of services to agro and to those who drive along the route. According to the latest census records (INDEC, 2010), this minor town grouped 509 inhabitants.

Los Ortiz site, on the other hand, is located 12 km from the city of Batan by a dirt road identified as los Ortiz road. It is a country road that runs through traditional General Pueyrredón District country estates, with old farmhouses, stud farms, milking yards, kiwi crops, as well as extensive production typical of the Pampean Argentine Region. It concentrates scattered rural population.

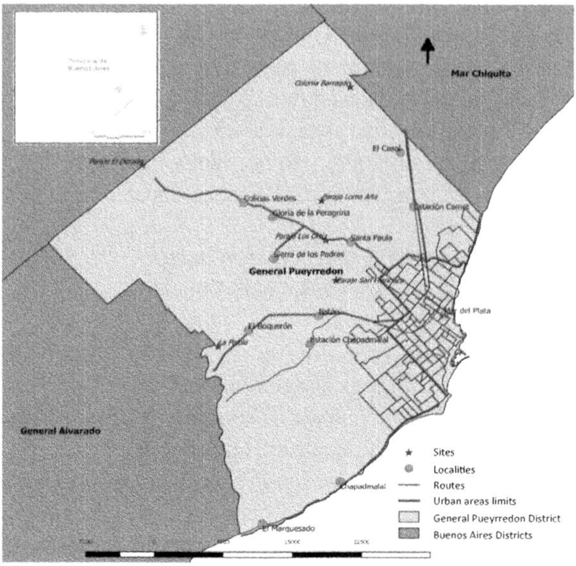

Fig. 7.1 General Pueyrredon District, localities. (Source: Author's elaboration)

7.5 Analysis

The analysis of the outlined questions makes it possible to establish preliminary ideas concerning 12-year-old participation in the rural area of General Pueyrredon District. The purpose is to retrieve a series of answers that characterize rural communities of El Boquerón (30 children) and Los Ortiz (66 children), allowing the possibility of finding some evidences regarding the participation and rights of these children.

At first, taking participation as a right, data related to the knowledge children have about it is resumed. As Hart (1993) emphasizes, the Convention on the Rights of the Child makes it plain to all that children are independent subjects and therefore have rights. But it is essential that they know these rights and also be responsible for them. In this sense, on the question 'I know the rights that children have' (Fig. 7.2), most of the cases respond in the affirmative, interpreting it as being one of the contents that are developed in the school curriculum. However, there are also children who hesitate in their answers. Data collected express that in Los Ortiz town, 46 children of the 66 enquired know the rights of the child and in El Boquerón town, 23 children of the 30 participants also know their rights.

Novella Cámara (2012), in referring to the Convention of Children's Rights poses three central axes, the first of them is the right of children to express their opinion and to be taken into account, the second concerns the importance of training them on their rights and the third contemplates the responsibility those rights imply to children. When researching them on the document that refers to their

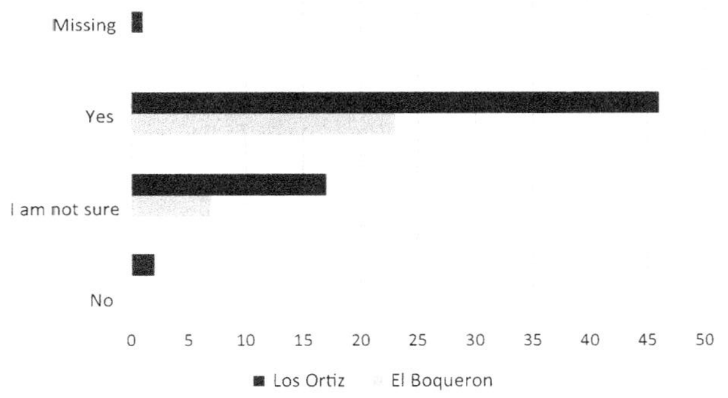

Fig. 7.2 I know the rights that children have. (Source: Own elaboration based on surveys made in Los Ortiz & El Boquerón, 2018)

rights, the scenario shows more doubts than certainties, since in both institutions, in most cases, answers show insecurity. In El Boquerón, 13 children are not sure to know the Convention, other 13 know it and 3 do not know it at all. In Los Ortiz, 31 children are not sure to know the Convention, 20 know it and 13 do not know it.

In reference to their opinions on the respect for the rights of the child in Argentina, it can be indicated that both groups of students *agree somewhat* with that statement (10 cases in El Boquerón and 24 cases in Los Ortiz) followed by *little agreement* (6 cases in El Boquerón and 15 cases in Los Ortiz).

In looking into the possibilities of making their decisions themselves in Argentina, the collected data warn that the vast majority *agree somewhat* (11 cases in El Boquerón and 22 cases in Los Ortiz), followed by *very little agreement* (5 cases in El Boquerón and 15 cases in Los Ortiz).

As Casas et al. (2008) expressed, quoting Apud (2001), the family is the first instance of socialization for the development of child participation. It has a fundamental role in the process of creating participatory skills and developing responsibilities.

On all the cases worked and in the field of their possibilities of making decisions together with adults, the children respond mostly to *agree* with those possibilities, especially in Los Ortiz, although in El Boquerón, there are similar answers between *completely agree* and *very little agreement*. In El Boquerón, out of the 30 children consulted, 10 *completely agree* and 10 *agree*, the rest is distributed among the other options. In Los Ortiz, on the other hand, 38 children *completely agree* and 15 *agree*, out of a total of 66.

However, when you ask them about the real opportunities for participation in decisions on issues concerning children, Fig. 7.3 reveals, in general, more responses to *disagreement* or denote that they *do not know*. In El Boquerón, 11

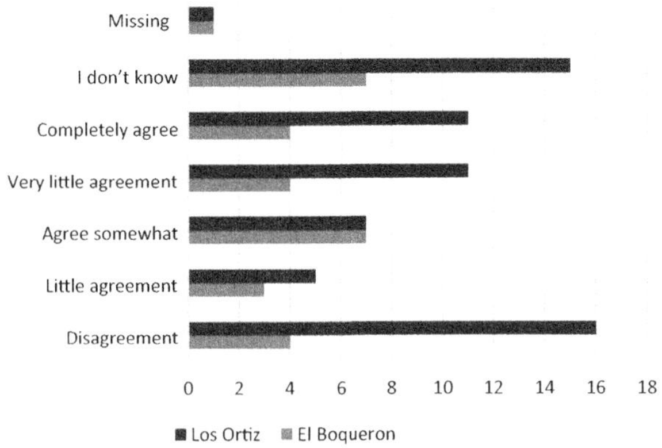

Fig. 7.3 Opportunities to participate in decisions. (Source: Own elaboration based on surveys made in Los Ortiz & El Boquerón, 2018)

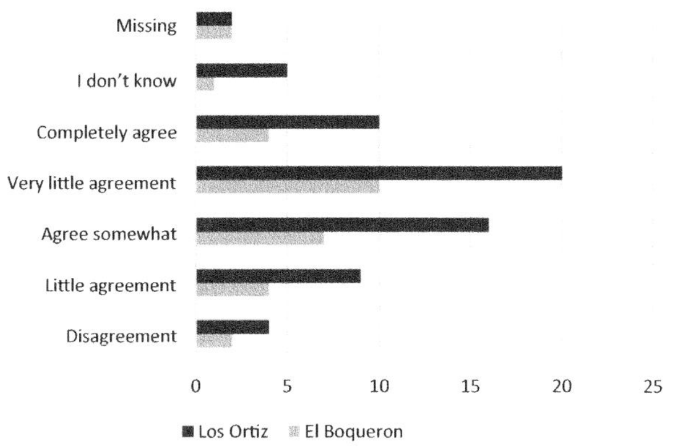

Fig. 7.4 My teachers listen to me and take into account what I say. (Source: Own elaboration based on surveys made in Los Ortiz & El Boquerón, 2018)

children respond to favor between *agree somewhat* and *very little agreement* and 7 *do not know*. Meanwhile, in Los Ortiz, 18 children express that they *agree somewhat* and *very little agreement*, along with 15 who *don't know*. It is in the places of residence of the various social groups where local states, organizations and families must specifically guarantee such participation.

Another set of adults with whom children spend a lot of time daily are their teachers. They were asked if they feel that their teachers take into account what they say. In both cases, *very little agreement* predominates (Fig. 7.4).

In line with Santiago (2014), we find, regarding participation in relation to teachers, that students embody a controlled participation, since children must do what teachers state. Generally, regarding their connections with the community, children express not being in agreement with the level of opportunities given for their participation. In this sense, the call for attention is given to the role of educational institutions, from which children do not agree to feel heard and taken into account.

Another sounding referred to the level of satisfaction on his own freedom and responsibilities.

Novella Cámara (2012) states that education is intended to train free people who feel and can express themselves and will be able to do so if they are allowed to experience freedom within the framework of family and community coexistence. On a scale of 0 to 10, where 0 means 'Not satisfied at all' and 10 'Completely satisfied'; the answers in reference to their freedom are mostly concentrated between values 8, 9 and 10, that is to say with a good degree of satisfaction in both studied spaces.

On the feature of responsibility, Novella Cámara (2012) proposes that children not only have the opportunity to be increasingly competent about their participation but as autonomous persons, they must work on recognizing their responsibilities and competences to define personal projects and also join collective projects.

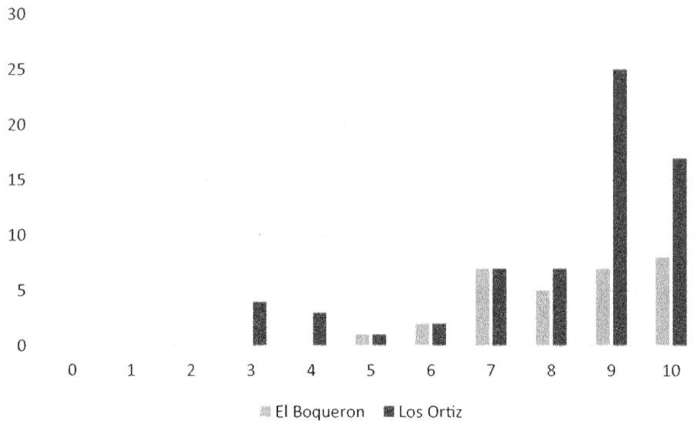

Fig. 7.5 I am good at managing my daily responsibilities. (Source: Own elaboration based on surveys made in Los Ortiz & El Boquerón, 2018)

Looking into the management of their own responsibilities, as shown in Fig. 7.5, on a scale of 0 to 10, the values in Los Ortiz are concentrated between 9 and 10 points, while in El Boquerón, the range goes between 7 and 10 points.

The education of children and the coexistence that takes place in families, educational institutions and society can be carried out to the extent that they learn to participate. The ability to participate reflects knowledge, skills, values, attitudes, conflict and skills that sustain the ability to demand information, training and responsibility.

Child participation must be an educational experience where children are involved as critical interpreters of their daily life and where dialogue and committed action are fundamental pillars (Novella Cámara, 2012, p. 390). To this end, the role of adults, educators, parents and institutions is essential by contributing to due knowledge and information on the right to participation in particular and on all rights in general.

7.6 Concluding Remarks

This chapter aimed to contribute to the discussion of rurality expressed in the role of South American children as subjects with rights in connection with their possibilities of participation.

The theoretical journey allowed to outline some first conceptual guidelines between rurality and participation. Likewise, the empirical journey provided first results on feeling and knowledge, regarding participation as a right consulted to rural children in the district of General Pueyrredon, administrative unit of the Province of Buenos Aires framed within the territories that make up the Southern Cone. From the rural setting, it is necessary to contribute to the study of the link between rurality and child participation. Rural inhabitants in general and children in particular are protagonists in this link.

The inhabitants of rural communities are active actors. This implies abandoning the residual definition of rurality as rurality has a complementary relationship with urbanity.

Educational institutions play a central role in strengthening this relationship. Evaluations and projects have been carried out to strengthen social actors related to participation in rural communities. However, there is an important gap in the methodologies of analysis, indicators and instruments to measure the development and trend of rural participation.

Therefore, this research shows that there is still a need to improve the design and implementation of new instruments that allow a qualitative look for the deepening of the proposed objective. Likewise it becomes interesting to consider the possibility of comparability among rural environments, and even between rurality and urbanity, bringing light to the link participation-residence space of children.

References

Abramovay, R. (2006) Para una teoría de los estudios territoriales. En Manzanal, M.; Neiman, G. y Lattuada, M. (orgs.) *Desarrollo rural: organizaciones, instituciones y territorios* (pp. 51–70). Ciccus.

Baylina, M., Ortiz, A., & y Prats, M. (2006). Geografía de la infancia: Espacios de juego en ciudades medias de Cataluña. *Geographicalia, 50*, 5–26.

Cámara, N., & María, A. (2012). La participación infantil: Concepto dimensional en pro de la autonomía ciudadana. *Teoría de la Educación. Educación y Cultura en la Sociedad de la Información, 13*(2), 380–403. Universidad de Salamanca Salamanca, España. http://campus.usal.es/~revistas_trabajo/index.php/revistatesi/article/view/9015/9259.

Casas, F., González, M., Carme, M., Navarro, D., Malo, S., Figuer, C., & y Bertran I. (2008). *Informe sobre experiencias de participación social efectiva de niños, niñas y Adolescentes.* Ministerio de Educación, Política Social y Deporte.

Castillo-Gallardo, P. (2015). Desigualdad e infancia: Lectura crítica de la Historia de la Infancia en Chile y en América Latina. *Revista Latinoamericana De Ciencias Sociales, Niñez y Juventud, 13*(1), 97–109.

Castro, J. (2009). Participación de niños, niñas y adolescentes a partir del espíritu y la letra de la convención, así como de las experiencias generadas en el contexto de su aplicación. En: Figueroa, E. (coord.). *Participación de los niños y niñas* (pp. 23–55). Ifejant.

Crowley, P. (1998). Participación infantil: Para una definición del marco conceptual. En UNICEF. La participación de niños y adolescentes en el contexto de la convención sobre los derechos del niño: visiones y perspectivas. Actas del seminario. Bogota 7–8 de diciembre de 1998.

Checkoway, B. (2011). What is youth participation? *Children and Youth Services Review, 33*(2), 340–345. https://doi.org/10.1016/j.childyouth.2010.09.017.

Gaudin, Y. (2019) *Nuevas narrativas para una transformación rural en América Latina y el Caribe. La nueva ruralidad: conceptos y medición.* Documentos de proyecto. Cepal-Fida.

González, F. (2015). La 'nueva ruralidad' en Cañuelas. Entre la agroecología y las nuevas urbanizaciones. *Mundo Agrario, 16*(31). Recuperado a partir de http://www.mundoagrario.unlp.edu.ar/article/view/MAv16n31a06.

Hart, R. (1993). La participación de los niños: de la participación simbolica a la participación autentica, *Innocenti Essay no. 4.* International Child Development Centre.

Holloway, S. (2014). Changing children's geographies. *Children's Geographies, 12*(4), 377–392. https://doi.org/10.1080/14733285.2014.930414.

Instituto Nacional de Estadística y Censos (INDEC). (2010). Censo Nacional de Población, Hogares y Viviendas de la Argentina https://www.indec.gob.ar/indec/web/Nivel3-Tema-2-41.

Jaramillo Garcia, E. (2018) Pensamiento social sobre la infancia: una mirada sociohistórica desde el sur global. *Discursos Del Sur, n.° 2*, julio/diciembre, 203–232 | https://doi.org/10.15381/dds.v0i2.15481.

Karsten, L. (2005). It all used to be better? Different generations on continuity and change in urban children's daily use of space. *Children's Geographies, 3*(3), 275–290.

Kay, C. (2016), La transformación neoliberal del mundo rural: procesos de concentración de la tierra y del capital y la intensificación de la precariedad del trabajo, *Revista Latinoamericana de Estudios Rurales, I (1)*. http://www.ceil-conicet.gov.ar/ojs/index.php/revistaalasru/article/view/93.

Kay, C. (2007). Algunas reflexiones sobre los estudios rurales en América Latina. Iconos. *Revista De Ciencias Sociales, 29,* 31–50.

Llambí Insua, L., & y Pérez Correa, E. (2007) Nuevas ruralidades y viejos campesinismos. Agenda para una nueva sociología rural latinoamericana *Cuadernos de Desarrollo Rural, núm. 59, julio-diciembre* (pp. 37–61). Pontificia Universidad Javeriana Bogóta.

Llambi, L. (2012). Procesos de transformación de los territorios rurales latinoamericanos: Los retos de la interdisciplinariedad. *Eutopia, 3,* 117–134.

Malatesta, S., & y Granados Sánchez, J. (2017). La contribución de la geografía de los niños y de las niñas a la enseñanza de la geografía. *Documents D'anàlisi Geogràfica, 63*(3), 631–640.

Mieles Barrera, M. D., & y Tonon, G. (2015). *Calidad de vida y niñez: Perspectivas desde la investigación cualitativa.* Universidad del Magdalena.

Mikkelsen, C. Sagua, M., Tomas, M. & y Massone, H. (2013) Dinámica socio-territorial de las localidades menores en el corredor Mar del Plata-Tandil (CMT). En: Revista Estudios Ambientales. CINEA. FCH. UNCPBA (pp. 67–85).

Moreira Lopes, J., & y de Vasconcellos, T. (2006). Geografia da infância: Territorialidades Infantis. *Currículo Sem Fronteiras, 6*(1), 103–127.

Nomura, B., & y Solari, G. (2005). Participación de niños, niñas y adolescentes a los 15 años de la Convención sobre los Derechos del Niño. Lima: Save the Children Suecia (Programa Regional para América Latina y El Caribe).

Ortiz Guitart, A. (2007). Geografías de la infancia: descubriendo «nuevas formas» de ver y de entender el mundo. *Doc. Anàl. Geogr. 49,* 197–216. https://ddd.uab.cat/pub/dag/02121573n49/02121573n49p197.pdf.

Ortiz Guitart, A., Prats Ferret, M., & y Baylina Ferré, M. (2012). Métodos visuales y geografías de la infancia: dibujando el entorno cotidiano. *Scripta Nova. Revista Electrónica de Geografía y Ciencias Sociales.* Universidad de Barcelona, *XVI*(400), 1–33. http://www.ub.es/geocrit/sn/sn-400.htm.

Phillips, R. (2001). Geographies of childhood: Introduction. *Area, 33,* 117–118. https://doi.org/10.1111/1475-4762.00014.

Ramirez Miranda, C. (2011). Critica al establishment del desarrollo en el campo: Nueva ruralidad y desarrollo territorial rural. *Estudios Latinoamericanos, Nueva Época, 14,* 107–128.

Santiago, R. (2014). Yo participo, tú participas, otra nos hace participar: La infancia y la autoría de su participación en la escuela. En: Calvo Salvador, A., Rodríguez-Hoyos, C. y Haya Salmón, H. (Coord.) *XIII Congreso Internacional de Formación del Profesorado. Investigar para acompañar el cambio educativo y social. El papel de la Universidad.* Asociación Universitaria de Formación del Profesorado (AUFOP) Universidad de Cantabria (pp. 14–24)

Tonon, G., Naón, G., & y Mikkelsen, C. (2018). Los proyectos de investigación desarrollados por UNICOM y LOMAS CYT que estudian la calidad de vida de niños y niñas. In: Tonon, G. (ed.) *Conocer la vida de niños y niñas desde las palabras de sus protagonistas.* Universidad Nacional de Lomas de Zamora.

Torres Victoria, N. (2008). La participación en las comunidades rurales: abriendo espacios para la participación desde la escuela. *Revista Educare XII, N° Extraordinario,* (pp. 115–119).

Urcola, M. (2011). Nueva ruralidad y contexto de globalización. *Regiones, suplemento de antropología, número 45,* junio-agosto de 2011, (pp. 6–11).

Valentine, G. (2004). Childhood in crisis? In: *Public space and the culture* (pp. 1–13). Routledge.

Valentine, G. (1996). Angels and devils: Moral landscapes of childhood. *Environment and Planning D: Society and Space, 14*(5), 581–599. https://doi.org/10.1068/d140581.

Printed by Printforce, the Netherlands